TEACHER'S PET PUBLICATIONS

PUZZLE PACK
for
Rumble Fish

based on the book by
S. E. Hinton

Written by
Mary B. Collins

© 2005 Teacher's Pet Publications
All Rights Reserved

The materials in this packet are copyrighted
by Teacher's Pet Publications, Inc.

These pages may be duplicated by the purchaser
for use in the purchaser's own classroom.

Copying any of these materials and distributing them
for any other purpose is a violation of the copyright laws.

© 2005 Teacher's Pet Publications, Inc.
www.tpet.com

INTRODUCTION
If you already own the LitPlan for this title, this Puzzle Pack will refresh your Unit Resource Materials and Vocabulary Resource Materials sections plus give you additional materials you can substitute into the tests. If you do not already have a complete LitPlan, these pages will give you some supplemental materials to use with your own plan. There are two main groups of materials: one set for unit words (such as characters' names, symbols, places, etc.) and one set for vocabulary words associated with the book.

WORD LIST
There is a word list for both the unit words and the vocabulary words. These lists show you which words are being used in the materials and the clues or definitions being used for those words. You may want to give students a word list with clues/definitions to help them, or you may want students to only have a word list (without clues/definitions) if you want them to work a little harder. Both are available for duplication. The word lists can also be your "calling key" for the bingo games.

FILL IN THE BLANK AND MATCHING
There are 4 each of the fill in the blank and matching worksheets for both the unit and vocabulary words. These pages can be used either as extra worksheets for students or as objective parts of a unit test. They can be done individually if students need extra help or as a whole class activity to review the material covered.

MAGIC SQUARES
The magic squares not only reinforce the material covered but also work on reasoning and math skills. Many teachers have told us that their students really enjoy doing these!

WORD SEARCH PUZZLES
The word search words go in all directions, as indicated on your answer keys. Two of the word search puzzles have the clues listed rather than the words. This makes the puzzle a little more difficult, but it reinforces the material better. Two word search puzzles have words only for students who find the clue puzzles too difficult.

CROSSWORD PUZZLES
Both unit and vocabulary word sections have 4 crossword puzzles.

BINGO CARDS
There are 32 individual bingo cards for the unit words and 32 individual bingo cards for the vocabulary words. You can use your word list as a "call list," calling the words at random and marking them off of your list as you go, or you could use the flash cards by cutting them apart and drawing the words at random from a hat (or box or whatever). To make a better review, you might ask for the definition and spelling of each word as you call it out–or you could call out the definitions and have students tell you the words they need to look for on the puzzle.

JUGGLE LETTERS
The vocabulary juggle letter game is intended to help students learn the spellings of the words. One sheet has the definitions listed on it as an extra help for students who need it or to reinforce the definitions if you choose to do so.

FLASH CARDS
We've included a set of vocabulary flash cards you can duplicate, cut, and fold for your students. Some teachers make a few sets for general use by the class; others make a set for each student. Some teachers duplicate them for each student and have the students cut & fold their own. You can cut out just the words and put them in a hat, have each student pick out one word and write the definition and a sentence for that word. Students then swap words and papers, with the next student adding a sentence of his own under the last one. You can have students swap as many times as you like. Each time the student will read the sentences written prior to his own and then add a sentence. You can cut out the words and definitions separately and play "I Have; Who Has?" Each student in the room draws a word and definition. The first student says, "I have (the name of the word). Who has the definition?" The student with the definition reads it then says, "I have (the name of the vocabulary word she has). Who has the definition?" The round continues until all words and definitions have been given.

Rumble Fish Word List

No.	Word	Clue/Definition
1.	ANITA	Rusty-James insulted her
2.	BEACH	Where the story started
3.	BENNY	Junior high hangout: ____'s
4.	BIFF	Knifed Rusty-James: ___ Wilcox
5.	BLIND	The Motorcycle Boy's condition: color ___
6.	BROTHER	Rusty-James wanted to be like his ___
7.	CALIFORNIA	The Motorcycle Boy went there
8.	CASSANDRA	Student teacher who liked the Motorcycle Boy
9.	CHEVY	The car with mag wheels
10.	CITY	Rusty-James liked the excitement there
11.	CLEVELAND	School Rusty-James did not want to attend
12.	DEVIL	Would have been Biff's gang: ___ Hawks
13.	DON	Coach wanted Rusty-James to beat him up
14.	DONNELY	Pet store owner
15.	DOPE	It ruined the gangs.
16.	HARRIGAN	Guidance counselor
17.	HOSPITAL	Steve's mother was there
18.	JACKSON	Fat, but tough: B. J. ___
19.	JEANNIE	She liked Steve but not Rusty-James: ___ Martin
20.	KNIFE	Bill's weapon
21.	LAWYER	Rusty-James's father was an ex-____ who drank all day
22.	LITTLE	Pee-wee branch of the local gang: ___ Leaguers
23.	LOYALTY	Rusty-James's only vice
24.	MAGAZINE	It had a picture of Motorcycle Boy
25.	MAGS	The hubcaps Rusty-James tried to steal
26.	MIDGET	Tallest boy in the crowd
27.	MILK	Rusty-James drank it before a fight: chocolate ___
28.	MOTORCYCLE	____ Boy didn't belong anywhere
29.	PACKERS	Local gang
30.	PAIN	It didn't scare Rusty-James
31.	PARROT	It said a lot of bad words
32.	PATTERSON	Police officer who shot the Motorcycle Boy
33.	PATTY	Rusty-James's girlfriend
34.	PET	The Motorcycle Boy broke into it: ___ store
35.	REFORMATORY	Rusty-James spent five years there
36.	ROOF	Rusty-James jumped from one to another
37.	RUMBLEFISH	Siamese fighting fish that killed each other
38.	RYAN	Coach who wanted Rusty-James to beat up a student
39.	SHOT	The Motorcycle Boy died from it
40.	SIAMESE	The Motorcycle Boy took the ___ flying fish to the river
41.	SIN	Steve didn't like the movies there: ___ City
42.	SMILE	The Motorcycle Boy's scared Rusty-James
43.	SMOKEY	Would have been the top tough guy
44.	SNEAKY	Rusty-James drank it a lot: ___ Pete
45.	STEVE	Rusty-James's best friend

Copyrighted

Rumble Fish Fill In The Blanks 1

_____
_____
_____
_____
_____
_____
_____
_____
_____
_____
_____
_____
_____
_____
_____
_____
_____
_____
_____
_____

1. ____ Boy didn't belong anywhere
2. Bill's weapon
3. Pee-wee branch of the local gang: ____ Leaguers
4. Would have been the top tough guy
5. Steve didn't like the movies there: ____ City
6. Rusty-James wanted to be like his ____
7. Local gang
8. Rusty-James's girlfriend
9. Rusty-James's father was an ex-____ who drank all day
10. Siamese fighting fish that killed each other
11. Rusty-James's only vice
12. It said a lot of bad words
13. The hubcaps Rusty-James tried to steal
14. The Motorcycle Boy died from it
15. The Motorcycle Boy took the ____ flying fish to the river
16. Police officer who shot the Motorcycle Boy
17. The Motorcycle Boy's scared Rusty-James
18. Rusty-James jumped from one to another
19. Tallest boy in the crowd
20. Would have been Biff's gang: ____ Hawks

Rumble Fish Fill In The Blanks 1 Answer Key

MOTORCYCLE	1. ____ Boy didn't belong anywhere
KNIFE	2. Bill's weapon
LITTLE	3. Pee-wee branch of the local gang: ____ Leaguers
SMOKEY	4. Would have been the top tough guy
SIN	5. Steve didn't like the movies there: ____ City
BROTHER	6. Rusty-James wanted to be like his ____
PACKERS	7. Local gang
PATTY	8. Rusty-James's girlfriend
LAWYER	9. Rusty-James's father was an ex-____ who drank all day
RUMBLEFISH	10. Siamese fighting fish that killed each other
LOYALTY	11. Rusty-James's only vice
PARROT	12. It said a lot of bad words
MAGS	13. The hubcaps Rusty-James tried to steal
SHOT	14. The Motorcycle Boy died from it
SIAMESE	15. The Motorcycle Boy took the ____ flying fish to the river
PATTERSON	16. Police officer who shot the Motorcycle Boy
SMILE	17. The Motorcycle Boy's scared Rusty-James
ROOF	18. Rusty-James jumped from one to another
MIDGET	19. Tallest boy in the crowd
DEVIL	20. Would have been Biff's gang: ____ Hawks

Rumble Fish Fill In The Blanks 2

_____ 1. Rusty-James liked the excitement there
_____ 2. Fat, but tough: B. J. ___
_____ 3. The Motorcycle Boy took the ___ flying fish to the river
_____ 4. Coach wanted Rusty-James to beat him up
_____ 5. Bill's weapon
_____ 6. Tallest boy in the crowd
_____ 7. The car with mag wheels
_____ 8. It had a picture of Motorcycle Boy
_____ 9. Steve's mother was there
_____ 10. Local gang
_____ 11. Steve didn't like the movies there: ___ City
_____ 12. The Motorcycle Boy died from it
_____ 13. Would have been Biff's gang: ___ Hawks
_____ 14. The Motorcycle Boy went there
_____ 15. Rusty-James's best friend
_____ 16. Rusty-James insulted her
_____ 17. It ruined the gangs.
_____ 18. School Rusty-James did not want to attend
_____ 19. She liked Steve but not Rusty-James: ___ Martin
_____ 20. Student teacher who liked the Motorcycle Boy

Rumble Fish Fill In The Blanks 2 Answer Key

CITY	1. Rusty-James liked the excitement there
JACKSON	2. Fat, but tough: B. J. ___
SIAMESE	3. The Motorcycle Boy took the ___ flying fish to the river
DON	4. Coach wanted Rusty-James to beat him up
KNIFE	5. Bill's weapon
MIDGET	6. Tallest boy in the crowd
CHEVY	7. The car with mag wheels
MAGAZINE	8. It had a picture of Motorcycle Boy
HOSPITAL	9. Steve's mother was there
PACKERS	10. Local gang
SIN	11. Steve didn't like the movies there: ___ City
SHOT	12. The Motorcycle Boy died from it
DEVIL	13. Would have been Biff's gang: ___ Hawks
CALIFORNIA	14. The Motorcycle Boy went there
STEVE	15. Rusty-James's best friend
ANITA	16. Rusty-James insulted her
DOPE	17. It ruined the gangs.
CLEVELAND	18. School Rusty-James did not want to attend
JEANNIE	19. She liked Steve but not Rusty-James: ___ Martin
CASSANDRA	20. Student teacher who liked the Motorcycle Boy

Rumble Fish Fill In The Blanks 3

_____ 1. Would have been Biff's gang: ___ Hawks

_____ 2. Rusty-James's girlfriend

_____ 3. It said a lot of bad words

_____ 4. The Motorcycle Boy's scared Rusty-James

_____ 5. The Motorcycle Boy went there

_____ 6. Guidance counselor

_____ 7. School Rusty-James did not want to attend

_____ 8. Rusty-James insulted her

_____ 9. Rusty-James wanted to be like his ___

_____ 10. Student teacher who liked the Motorcycle Boy

_____ 11. Where the story started

_____ 12. Rusty-James drank it a lot: ___ Pete

_____ 13. The Motorcycle Boy's condition: color ___

_____ 14. Knifed Rusty-James: ___ Wilcox

_____ 15. Would have been the top tough guy

_____ 16. Rusty-James drank it before a fight: chocolate ___

_____ 17. Junior high hangout: ____'s

_____ 18. Rusty-James's only vice

_____ 19. Rusty-James liked the excitement there

_____ 20. The Motorcycle Boy took the ___ flying fish to the river

Rumble Fish Fill In The Blanks 3 Answer Key

DEVIL	1. Would have been Biff's gang: ___ Hawks
PATTY	2. Rusty-James's girlfriend
PARROT	3. It said a lot of bad words
SMILE	4. The Motorcycle Boy's scared Rusty-James
CALIFORNIA	5. The Motorcycle Boy went there
HARRIGAN	6. Guidance counselor
CLEVELAND	7. School Rusty-James did not want to attend
ANITA	8. Rusty-James insulted her
BROTHER	9. Rusty-James wanted to be like his ___
CASSANDRA	10. Student teacher who liked the Motorcycle Boy
BEACH	11. Where the story started
SNEAKY	12. Rusty-James drank it a lot: ___ Pete
BLIND	13. The Motorcycle Boy's condition: color ___
BIFF	14. Knifed Rusty-James: ___ Wilcox
SMOKEY	15. Would have been the top tough guy
MILK	16. Rusty-James drank it before a fight: chocolate ___
BENNY	17. Junior high hangout: ____'s
LOYALTY	18. Rusty-James's only vice
CITY	19. Rusty-James liked the excitement there
SIAMESE	20. The Motorcycle Boy took the ___ flying fish to the river

Rumble Fish Fill In The Blanks 4

_____

1. Rusty-James wanted to be like his ___
2. The Motorcycle Boy went there
3. Tallest boy in the crowd
4. School Rusty-James did not want to attend
5. Student teacher who liked the Motorcycle Boy
6. Rusty-James's best friend
7. Rusty-James spent five years there
8. It had a picture of Motorcycle Boy
9. Pet store owner
10. Rusty-James's father was an ex-____ who drank all day
11. Siamese fighting fish that killed each other
12. The hubcaps Rusty-James tried to steal
13. Where the story started
14. Coach who wanted Rusty-James to beat up a student
15. Local gang
16. Pee-wee branch of the local gang: ___ Leaguers
17. It said a lot of bad words
18. Rusty-James jumped from one to another
19. Guidance counselor
20. The Motorcycle Boy took the ___ flying fish to the river

Rumble Fish Fill In The Blanks 4 Answer Key

BROTHER	1. Rusty-James wanted to be like his ___
CALIFORNIA	2. The Motorcycle Boy went there
MIDGET	3. Tallest boy in the crowd
CLEVELAND	4. School Rusty-James did not want to attend
CASSANDRA	5. Student teacher who liked the Motorcycle Boy
STEVE	6. Rusty-James's best friend
REFORMATORY	7. Rusty-James spent five years there
MAGAZINE	8. It had a picture of Motorcycle Boy
DONNELY	9. Pet store owner
LAWYER	10. Rusty-James's father was an ex-____ who drank all day
RUMBLEFISH	11. Siamese fighting fish that killed each other
MAGS	12. The hubcaps Rusty-James tried to steal
BEACH	13. Where the story started
RYAN	14. Coach who wanted Rusty-James to beat up a student
PACKERS	15. Local gang
LITTLE	16. Pee-wee branch of the local gang: ___ Leaguers
PARROT	17. It said a lot of bad words
ROOF	18. Rusty-James jumped from one to another
HARRIGAN	19. Guidance counselor
SIAMESE	20. The Motorcycle Boy took the ___ flying fish to the river

Rumble Fish Matching 1

___ 1. KNIFE   A. Pee-wee branch of the local gang: ___ Leaguers
___ 2. CITY   B. It ruined the gangs.
___ 3. BEACH   C. The car with mag wheels
___ 4. CALIFORNIA   D. Steve's mother was there
___ 5. LOYALTY   E. The Motorcycle Boy went there
___ 6. SMILE   F. Police officer who shot the Motorcycle Boy
___ 7. LITTLE   G. Rusty-James's only vice
___ 8. BIFF   H. Rusty-James jumped from one to another
___ 9. RUMBLEFISH   I. It had a picture of Motorcycle Boy
___10. ANITA   J. It said a lot of bad words
___11. MOTORCYCLE   K. Bill's weapon
___12. DOPE   L. Student teacher who liked the Motorcycle Boy
___13. LAWYER   M. Rusty-James insulted her
___14. CHEVY   N. Rusty-James's father was an ex-____ who drank all day
___15. JEANNIE   O. The Motorcycle Boy's scared Rusty-James
___16. JACKSON   P. Would have been the top tough guy
___17. SMOKEY   Q. Rusty-James liked the excitement there
___18. STEVE   R. Knifed Rusty-James: ___ Wilcox
___19. MAGAZINE   S. Local gang
___20. ROOF   T. She liked Steve but not Rusty-James: ___ Martin
___21. CASSANDRA   U. Fat, but tough: B. J. ___
___22. PATTERSON   V. Rusty-James's best friend
___23. HOSPITAL   W. Where the story started
___24. PARROT   X. ____ Boy didn't belong anywhere
___25. PACKERS   Y. Siamese fighting fish that killed each other

Rumble Fish Matching 1 Answer Key

K - 1. KNIFE	A. Pee-wee branch of the local gang: ___ Leaguers
Q - 2. CITY	B. It ruined the gangs.
W - 3. BEACH	C. The car with mag wheels
E - 4. CALIFORNIA	D. Steve's mother was there
G - 5. LOYALTY	E. The Motorcycle Boy went there
O - 6. SMILE	F. Police officer who shot the Motorcycle Boy
A - 7. LITTLE	G. Rusty-James's only vice
R - 8. BIFF	H. Rusty-James jumped from one to another
Y - 9. RUMBLEFISH	I. It had a picture of Motorcycle Boy
M -10. ANITA	J. It said a lot of bad words
X -11. MOTORCYCLE	K. Bill's weapon
B -12. DOPE	L. Student teacher who liked the Motorcycle Boy
N -13. LAWYER	M. Rusty-James insulted her
C -14. CHEVY	N. Rusty-James's father was an ex-____ who drank all day
T -15. JEANNIE	O. The Motorcycle Boy's scared Rusty-James
U -16. JACKSON	P. Would have been the top tough guy
P -17. SMOKEY	Q. Rusty-James liked the excitement there
V -18. STEVE	R. Knifed Rusty-James: ___ Wilcox
I - 19. MAGAZINE	S. Local gang
H -20. ROOF	T. She liked Steve but not Rusty-James: ___ Martin
L -21. CASSANDRA	U. Fat, but tough: B. J. ___
F -22. PATTERSON	V. Rusty-James's best friend
D -23. HOSPITAL	W. Where the story started
J -24. PARROT	X. ___ Boy didn't belong anywhere
S -25. PACKERS	Y. Siamese fighting fish that killed each other

Rumble Fish Matching 2

___ 1. LITTLE
___ 2. REFORMATORY
___ 3. SHOT
___ 4. BENNY
___ 5. RYAN
___ 6. BLIND
___ 7. SMILE
___ 8. BROTHER
___ 9. SIAMESE
___10. CASSANDRA
___11. STEVE
___12. DEVIL
___13. PET
___14. MAGAZINE
___15. BEACH
___16. MAGS
___17. DOPE
___18. CLEVELAND
___19. KNIFE
___20. BIFF
___21. MOTORCYCLE
___22. PATTERSON
___23. RUMBLEFISH
___24. SMOKEY
___25. MILK

A. Bill's weapon
B. Student teacher who liked the Motorcycle Boy
C. Junior high hangout: ____'s
D. The hubcaps Rusty-James tried to steal
E. Police officer who shot the Motorcycle Boy
F. Rusty-James drank it before a fight: chocolate ___
G. The Motorcycle Boy's scared Rusty-James
H. The Motorcycle Boy took the ___ flying fish to the river
I. The Motorcycle Boy died from it
J. Coach who wanted Rusty-James to beat up a student
K. Pee-wee branch of the local gang: ___ Leaguers
L. School Rusty-James did not want to attend
M. Knifed Rusty-James: ___ Wilcox
N. Siamese fighting fish that killed each other
O. The Motorcycle Boy broke into it: ___ store
P. Would have been the top tough guy
Q. Rusty-James wanted to be like his ___
R. Where the story started
S. The Motorcycle Boy's condition: color ___
T. It had a picture of Motorcycle Boy
U. Rusty-James spent five years there
V. ____ Boy didn't belong anywhere
W. Would have been Biff's gang: ___ Hawks
X. Rusty-James's best friend
Y. It ruined the gangs.

Rumble Fish Matching 2 Answer Key

K - 1. LITTLE	A.	Bill's weapon
U - 2. REFORMATORY	B.	Student teacher who liked the Motorcycle Boy
I - 3. SHOT	C.	Junior high hangout: ____'s
C - 4. BENNY	D.	The hubcaps Rusty-James tried to steal
J - 5. RYAN	E.	Police officer who shot the Motorcycle Boy
S - 6. BLIND	F.	Rusty-James drank it before a fight: chocolate ___
G - 7. SMILE	G.	The Motorcycle Boy's scared Rusty-James
Q - 8. BROTHER	H.	The Motorcycle Boy took the ___ flying fish to the river
H - 9. SIAMESE	I.	The Motorcycle Boy died from it
B - 10. CASSANDRA	J.	Coach who wanted Rusty-James to beat up a student
X - 11. STEVE	K.	Pee-wee branch of the local gang: ___ Leaguers
W - 12. DEVIL	L.	School Rusty-James did not want to attend
O - 13. PET	M.	Knifed Rusty-James: ___ Wilcox
T - 14. MAGAZINE	N.	Siamese fighting fish that killed each other
R - 15. BEACH	O.	The Motorcycle Boy broke into it: ___ store
D - 16. MAGS	P.	Would have been the top tough guy
Y - 17. DOPE	Q.	Rusty-James wanted to be like his ___
L - 18. CLEVELAND	R.	Where the story started
A - 19. KNIFE	S.	The Motorcycle Boy's condition: color ___
M - 20. BIFF	T.	It had a picture of Motorcycle Boy
V - 21. MOTORCYCLE	U.	Rusty-James spent five years there
E - 22. PATTERSON	V.	___ Boy didn't belong anywhere
N - 23. RUMBLEFISH	W.	Would have been Biff's gang: ___ Hawks
P - 24. SMOKEY	X.	Rusty-James's best friend
F - 25. MILK	Y.	It ruined the gangs.

Rumble Fish Matching 3

___ 1. STEVE	A. Guidance counselor
___ 2. PARROT	B. It ruined the gangs.
___ 3. MILK	C. She liked Steve but not Rusty-James: ___ Martin
___ 4. DOPE	D. The Motorcycle Boy's condition: color ___
___ 5. CASSANDRA	E. Knifed Rusty-James: ___ Wilcox
___ 6. HOSPITAL	F. Where the story started
___ 7. LAWYER	G. Rusty-James's only vice
___ 8. JACKSON	H. It didn't scare Rusty-James
___ 9. REFORMATORY	I. Pet store owner
___10. LOYALTY	J. Rusty-James spent five years there
___11. BLIND	K. Student teacher who liked the Motorcycle Boy
___12. CITY	L. Would have been Biff's gang: ___ Hawks
___13. SIN	M. Rusty-James's girlfriend
___14. JEANNIE	N. Rusty-James drank it before a fight: chocolate ___
___15. PAIN	O. Rusty-James jumped from one to another
___16. PATTY	P. The hubcaps Rusty-James tried to steal
___17. SMILE	Q. Steve didn't like the movies there: ___ City
___18. BIFF	R. The Motorcycle Boy's scared Rusty-James
___19. ROOF	S. Fat, but tough: B. J. ___
___20. PET	T. The Motorcycle Boy broke into it: ___ store
___21. HARRIGAN	U. Rusty-James's best friend
___22. DEVIL	V. Rusty-James liked the excitement there
___23. BEACH	W. It said a lot of bad words
___24. MAGS	X. Steve's mother was there
___25. DONNELY	Y. Rusty-James's father was an ex-___ who drank all day

Rumble Fish Matching 3 Answer Key

U - 1.	STEVE	A. Guidance counselor
W - 2.	PARROT	B. It ruined the gangs.
N - 3.	MILK	C. She liked Steve but not Rusty-James: ___ Martin
B - 4.	DOPE	D. The Motorcycle Boy's condition: color ___
K - 5.	CASSANDRA	E. Knifed Rusty-James: ___ Wilcox
X - 6.	HOSPITAL	F. Where the story started
Y - 7.	LAWYER	G. Rusty-James's only vice
S - 8.	JACKSON	H. It didn't scare Rusty-James
J - 9.	REFORMATORY	I. Pet store owner
G -10.	LOYALTY	J. Rusty-James spent five years there
D -11.	BLIND	K. Student teacher who liked the Motorcycle Boy
V -12.	CITY	L. Would have been Biff's gang: ___ Hawks
Q -13.	SIN	M. Rusty-James's girlfriend
C -14.	JEANNIE	N. Rusty-James drank it before a fight: chocolate ___
H -15.	PAIN	O. Rusty-James jumped from one to another
M -16.	PATTY	P. The hubcaps Rusty-James tried to steal
R -17.	SMILE	Q. Steve didn't like the movies there: ___ City
E -18.	BIFF	R. The Motorcycle Boy's scared Rusty-James
O -19.	ROOF	S. Fat, but tough: B. J. ___
T -20.	PET	T. The Motorcycle Boy broke into it: ___ store
A -21.	HARRIGAN	U. Rusty-James's best friend
L -22.	DEVIL	V. Rusty-James liked the excitement there
F -23.	BEACH	W. It said a lot of bad words
P -24.	MAGS	X. Steve's mother was there
I -25.	DONNELY	Y. Rusty-James's father was an ex-____ who drank all day

Rumble Fish Matching 4

___ 1. SMOKEY A. Coach who wanted Rusty-James to beat up a student
___ 2. DONNELY B. Guidance counselor
___ 3. PAIN C. The Motorcycle Boy broke into it: ___ store
___ 4. PARROT D. Rusty-James drank it before a fight: chocolate ___
___ 5. MOTORCYCLE E. Bill's weapon
___ 6. MAGS F. It didn't scare Rusty-James
___ 7. JACKSON G. Rusty-James drank it a lot: ___ Pete
___ 8. SMILE H. Rusty-James's girlfriend
___ 9. MILK I. Rusty-James liked the excitement there
___ 10. CITY J. Police officer who shot the Motorcycle Boy
___ 11. SNEAKY K. Rusty-James spent five years there
___ 12. PACKERS L. The Motorcycle Boy went there
___ 13. PATTY M. Rusty-James's only vice
___ 14. MIDGET N. Would have been the top tough guy
___ 15. KNIFE O. It had a picture of Motorcycle Boy
___ 16. HARRIGAN P. The Motorcycle Boy's scared Rusty-James
___ 17. PET Q. Local gang
___ 18. MAGAZINE R. Rusty-James's father was an ex-___ who drank all day
___ 19. RYAN S. Pet store owner
___ 20. SHOT T. The hubcaps Rusty-James tried to steal
___ 21. PATTERSON U. The Motorcycle Boy died from it
___ 22. LOYALTY V. Tallest boy in the crowd
___ 23. CALIFORNIA W. Fat, but tough: B. J. ___
___ 24. REFORMATORY X. ___ Boy didn't belong anywhere
___ 25. LAWYER Y. It said a lot of bad words

Rumble Fish Matching 4 Answer Key

N - 1. SMOKEY	A.	Coach who wanted Rusty-James to beat up a student
S - 2. DONNELY	B.	Guidance counselor
F - 3. PAIN	C.	The Motorcycle Boy broke into it: ___ store
Y - 4. PARROT	D.	Rusty-James drank it before a fight: chocolate ___
X - 5. MOTORCYCLE	E.	Bill's weapon
T - 6. MAGS	F.	It didn't scare Rusty-James
W - 7. JACKSON	G.	Rusty-James drank it a lot: ___ Pete
P - 8. SMILE	H.	Rusty-James's girlfriend
D - 9. MILK	I.	Rusty-James liked the excitement there
I - 10. CITY	J.	Police officer who shot the Motorcycle Boy
G - 11. SNEAKY	K.	Rusty-James spent five years there
Q - 12. PACKERS	L.	The Motorcycle Boy went there
H - 13. PATTY	M.	Rusty-James's only vice
V - 14. MIDGET	N.	Would have been the top tough guy
E - 15. KNIFE	O.	It had a picture of Motorcycle Boy
B - 16. HARRIGAN	P.	The Motorcycle Boy's scared Rusty-James
C - 17. PET	Q.	Local gang
O - 18. MAGAZINE	R.	Rusty-James's father was an ex-___ who drank all day
A - 19. RYAN	S.	Pet store owner
U - 20. SHOT	T.	The hubcaps Rusty-James tried to steal
J - 21. PATTERSON	U.	The Motorcycle Boy died from it
M - 22. LOYALTY	V.	Tallest boy in the crowd
L - 23. CALIFORNIA	W.	Fat, but tough: B. J. ___
K - 24. REFORMATORY	X.	___ Boy didn't belong anywhere
R - 25. LAWYER	Y.	It said a lot of bad words

Copyrighted

Rumble Fish magic Squares 1

Match the definition with the vocabulary word. Put your answers in the magic squares below. When your answers are correct, all columns and rows will add to the same number.

A. DOPE	E. HARRIGAN	I. PET	M. MAGAZINE
B. BROTHER	F. BIFF	J. SIAMESE	N. REFORMATORY
C. RYAN	G. JACKSON	K. BEACH	O. BLIND
D. PACKERS	H. DONNELY	L. RUMBLEFISH	P. MIDGET

1. Pet store owner
2. It ruined the gangs.
3. Rusty-James wanted to be like his ___
4. Fat, but tough: B. J. ___
5. The Motorcycle Boy took the ___ flying fish to the river
6. The Motorcycle Boy's condition: color ___
7. Tallest boy in the crowd
8. The Motorcycle Boy broke into it: ___ store
9. Where the story started
10. Rusty-James spent five years there
11. It had a picture of Motorcycle Boy
12. Siamese fighting fish that killed each other
13. Guidance counselor
14. Local gang
15. Coach who wanted Rusty-James to beat up a student
16. Knifed Rusty-James: ___ Wilcox

A=	B=	C=	D=
E=	F=	G=	H=
I=	J=	K=	L=
M=	N=	O=	P=

Rumble Fish magic Squares 1 Answer Key

Match the definition with the vocabulary word. Put your answers in the magic squares below. When your answers are correct, all columns and rows will add to the same number.

A. DOPE
B. BROTHER
C. RYAN
D. PACKERS
E. HARRIGAN
F. BIFF
G. JACKSON
H. DONNELY
I. PET
J. SIAMESE
K. BEACH
L. RUMBLEFISH
M. MAGAZINE
N. REFORMATORY
O. BLIND
P. MIDGET

1. Pet store owner
2. It ruined the gangs.
3. Rusty-James wanted to be like his ___
4. Fat, but tough: B. J. ___
5. The Motorcycle Boy took the ___ flying fish to the river
6. The Motorcycle Boy's condition: color ___
7. Tallest boy in the crowd
8. The Motorcycle Boy broke into it: ___ store
9. Where the story started
10. Rusty-James spent five years there
11. It had a picture of Motorcycle Boy
12. Siamese fighting fish that killed each other
13. Guidance counselor
14. Local gang
15. Coach who wanted Rusty-James to beat up a student
16. Knifed Rusty-James: ___ Wilcox

A=2	B=3	C=15	D=14
E=13	F=16	G=4	H=1
I=8	J=5	K=9	L=12
M=11	N=10	O=6	P=7

22
Copyrighted

Rumble Fish magic Squares 2

Match the definition with the vocabulary word. Put your answers in the magic squares below. When your answers are correct, all columns and rows will add to the same number.

A. HOSPITAL
B. ROOF
C. BROTHER
D. PACKERS
E. PATTY
F. DON
G. MIDGET
H. RYAN
I. DONNELY
J. MAGS
K. BENNY
L. MAGAZINE
M. HARRIGAN
N. MOTORCYCLE
O. LAWYER
P. LITTLE

1. Rusty-James wanted to be like his ___
2. The hubcaps Rusty-James tried to steal
3. Coach wanted Rusty-James to beat him up
4. Rusty-James's father was an ex-___ who drank all day
5. Pee-wee branch of the local gang: ___ Leaguers
6. Rusty-James's girlfriend
7. Pet store owner
8. Local gang
9. Guidance counselor
10. Coach who wanted Rusty-James to beat up a student
11. It had a picture of Motorcycle Boy
12. Steve's mother was there
13. Rusty-James jumped from one to another
14. Junior high hangout: ___'s
15. Tallest boy in the crowd
16. ___ Boy didn't belong anywhere

A=	B=	C=	D=
E=	F=	G=	H=
I=	J=	K=	L=
M=	N=	O=	P=

Rumble Fish magic Squares 2 Answer Key

Match the definition with the vocabulary word. Put your answers in the magic squares below. When your answers are correct, all columns and rows will add to the same number.

A. HOSPITAL
B. ROOF
C. BROTHER
D. PACKERS
E. PATTY
F. DON
G. MIDGET
H. RYAN
I. DONNELY
J. MAGS
K. BENNY
L. MAGAZINE
M. HARRIGAN
N. MOTORCYCLE
O. LAWYER
P. LITTLE

1. Rusty-James wanted to be like his ___
2. The hubcaps Rusty-James tried to steal
3. Coach wanted Rusty-James to beat him up
4. Rusty-James's father was an ex-____ who drank all day
5. Pee-wee branch of the local gang: ___ Leaguers
6. Rusty-James's girlfriend
7. Pet store owner
8. Local gang
9. Guidance counselor
10. Coach who wanted Rusty-James to beat up a student
11. It had a picture of Motorcycle Boy
12. Steve's mother was there
13. Rusty-James jumped from one to another
14. Junior high hangout: ____'s
15. Tallest boy in the crowd
16. ____ Boy didn't belong anywhere

A=12	B=13	C=1	D=8
E=6	F=3	G=15	H=10
I=7	J=2	K=14	L=11
M=9	N=16	O=4	P=5

Rumble Fish magic Squares 3

Match the definition with the vocabulary word. Put your answers in the magic squares below. When your answers are correct, all columns and rows will add to the same number.

A. RUMBLEFISH
B. SNEAKY
C. BEACH
D. CASSANDRA
E. JEANNIE
F. SIAMESE
G. DONNELY
H. DOPE
I. PACKERS
J. MAGAZINE
K. BIFF
L. HOSPITAL
M. STEVE
N. BLIND
O. MAGS
P. SIN

1. Siamese fighting fish that killed each other
2. The Motorcycle Boy's condition: color ___
3. It had a picture of Motorcycle Boy
4. She liked Steve but not Rusty-James: ___ Martin
5. Pet store owner
6. Steve's mother was there
7. Steve didn't like the movies there: ___ City
8. Where the story started
9. The hubcaps Rusty-James tried to steal
10. Student teacher who liked the Motorcycle Boy
11. It ruined the gangs.
12. Knifed Rusty-James: ___ Wilcox
13. Local gang
14. The Motorcycle Boy took the ___ flying fish to the river
15. Rusty-James drank it a lot: ___ Pete
16. Rusty-James's best friend

A=	B=	C=	D=
E=	F=	G=	H=
I=	J=	K=	L=
M=	N=	O=	P=

Rumble Fish magic Squares 3 Answer Key

Match the definition with the vocabulary word. Put your answers in the magic squares below. When your answers are correct, all columns and rows will add to the same number.

A. RUMBLEFISH
B. SNEAKY
C. BEACH
D. CASSANDRA
E. JEANNIE
F. SIAMESE
G. DONNELY
H. DOPE
I. PACKERS
J. MAGAZINE
K. BIFF
L. HOSPITAL
M. STEVE
N. BLIND
O. MAGS
P. SIN

1. Siamese fighting fish that killed each other
2. The Motorcycle Boy's condition: color ___
3. It had a picture of Motorcycle Boy
4. She liked Steve but not Rusty-James: ___ Martin
5. Pet store owner
6. Steve's mother was there
7. Steve didn't like the movies there: ___ City
8. Where the story started
9. The hubcaps Rusty-James tried to steal
10. Student teacher who liked the Motorcycle Boy
11. It ruined the gangs.
12. Knifed Rusty-James: ___ Wilcox
13. Local gang
14. The Motorcycle Boy took the ___ flying fish to the river
15. Rusty-James drank it a lot: ___ Pete
16. Rusty-James's best friend

A=1	B=15	C=8	D=10
E=4	F=14	G=5	H=11
I=13	J=3	K=12	L=6
M=16	N=2	O=9	P=7

Rumble Fish magic Squares 4

Match the definition with the vocabulary word. Put your answers in the magic squares below. When your answers are correct, all columns and rows will add to the same number.

A. JACKSON
B. MAGAZINE
C. JEANNIE
D. ANITA
E. SMOKEY
F. DONNELY
G. HARRIGAN
H. SIN
I. SIAMESE
J. SNEAKY
K. LITTLE
L. DOPE
M. CITY
N. BLIND
O. LAWYER
P. BROTHER

1. Steve didn't like the movies there: ___ City
2. Rusty-James liked the excitement there
3. It had a picture of Motorcycle Boy
4. Pee-wee branch of the local gang: ___ Leaguers
5. Rusty-James drank it a lot: ___ Pete
6. She liked Steve but not Rusty-James: ___ Martin
7. Rusty-James wanted to be like his ___
8. Would have been the top tough guy
9. Rusty-James's father was an ex-___ who drank all day
10. Pet store owner
11. The Motorcycle Boy took the ___ flying fish to the river
12. Rusty-James insulted her
13. Fat, but tough: B. J. ___
14. It ruined the gangs.
15. Guidance counselor
16. The Motorcycle Boy's condition: color ___

A=	B=	C=	D=
E=	F=	G=	H=
I=	J=	K=	L=
M=	N=	O=	P=

Rumble Fish magic Squares 4 Answer Key

Match the definition with the vocabulary word. Put your answers in the magic squares below. When your answers are correct, all columns and rows will add to the same number.

A. JACKSON
B. MAGAZINE
C. JEANNIE
D. ANITA
E. SMOKEY
F. DONNELY
G. HARRIGAN
H. SIN
I. SIAMESE
J. SNEAKY
K. LITTLE
L. DOPE
M. CITY
N. BLIND
O. LAWYER
P. BROTHER

1. Steve didn't like the movies there: ___ City
2. Rusty-James liked the excitement there
3. It had a picture of Motorcycle Boy
4. Pee-wee branch of the local gang: ___ Leaguers
5. Rusty-James drank it a lot: ___ Pete
6. She liked Steve but not Rusty-James: ___ Martin
7. Rusty-James wanted to be like his ___
8. Would have been the top tough guy
9. Rusty-James's father was an ex-___ who drank all day
10. Pet store owner
11. The Motorcycle Boy took the ___ flying fish to the river
12. Rusty-James insulted her
13. Fat, but tough: B. J. ___
14. It ruined the gangs.
15. Guidance counselor
16. The Motorcycle Boy's condition: color ___

A=13	B=3	C=6	D=12
A=13	B=3	C=6	D=12
E=8	F=10	G=15	H=1
I=11	J=5	K=4	L=14
M=2	N=16	O=9	P=7

Rumble Fish Word Search 1

```
M O T O R C Y C L E J S R E K C A P J N
A M M G J F T F I B Q H N O S K C A J T
G N X N W S M B Q T R W A C J L V R Z R
A C Q F L I B P R R Y O F R S T T R C V
Z M B H G A R Z J S D G T Q R J X O K S
I R I C P M T Z C M F H F H I F T R N
N U N D B E G P D N G D R O E F G Z Y H
E M O V G S B K O F F O S N C R X A P
H B S P P E T L N I A P P Z L B L I N D
F L R V L V T I N I I E R I E A K C I S
X E E T L E S Z L T F T V X V Y W M T Z
K F T T Q T N X A C N E Y S E M C Y A V
Q I T P G S B L L M D V A F L W A P E N
L S A T M F N E P P I R Y C A X L G T R
C H P I Q D C E N M D L E J N T I C S M
L H L Z P E O Y A N H Q K L D F F I B F
R E E L J I H N A K Y V O Q M X O S X G
K O W V L N G S N P Y Y M N R G R B H F
Z M O C Y N S F Z E A Y S S S P N E H V
F Y M F D A X G G L L T X B H Z I A R D
S V S Q C E N L T P J Y T F W O A C J M
D Z W Y L J Y Y Y D R D Q Y T Y T H W V
Q F Y V J K X N X D B T Q C G T H F X L
```

Bill's weapon (5)
Coach wanted Rusty-James to beat him up (3)
Coach who wanted Rusty-James to beat up a student (4)
Fat, but tough: B. J. ___ (7)
Guidance counselor (8)
It didn't scare Rusty-James (4)
It had a picture of Motorcycle Boy (8)
It ruined the gangs. (4)
It said a lot of bad words (6)
Junior high hangout: ____'s (5)
Knifed Rusty-James: ___ Wilcox (4)
Local gang (7)
Pee-wee branch of the local gang: ___ Leaguers (6)
Pet store owner (7)
Police officer who shot the Motorcycle Boy (9)
Rusty-James drank it a lot: ___ Pete (6)
Rusty-James drank it before a fight: chocolate ___ (4)
Rusty-James insulted her (5)
Rusty-James jumped from one to another (4)
Rusty-James liked the excitement there (4)
Rusty-James wanted to be like his ___ (7)
Rusty-James's best friend (5)
Rusty-James's father was an ex-____ who drank all day (6)
Rusty-James's girlfriend (5)
Rusty-James's only vice (7)
School Rusty-James did not want to attend (9)
She liked Steve but not Rusty-James: ___ Martin (7)
Siamese fighting fish that killed each other (10)
Steve didn't like the movies there: ___ City (3)
Steve's mother was there (8)
Student teacher who liked the Motorcycle Boy (9)
Tallest boy in the crowd (6)
The Motorcycle Boy broke into it: ___ store (3)
The Motorcycle Boy died from it (4)
The Motorcycle Boy took the ___ flying fish to the river (7)
The Motorcycle Boy went there (10)
The Motorcycle Boy's condition: color ___ (5)
The Motorcycle Boy's scared Rusty-James (5)
The car with mag wheels (5)
The hubcaps Rusty-James tried to steal (4)
Where the story started (5)
Would have been Biff's gang: ___ Hawks (5)
Would have been the top tough guy (6)
____ Boy didn't belong anywhere (10)

Rumble Fish Word Search 1 Answer Key

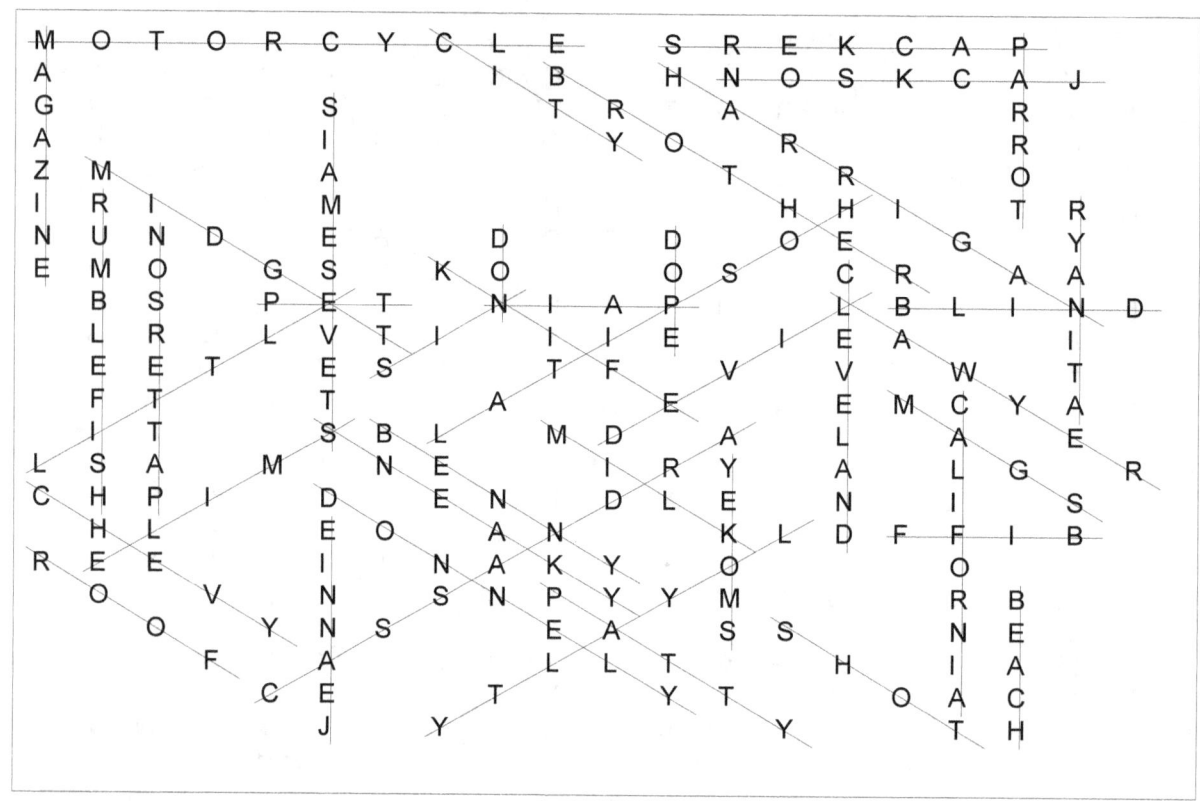

Bill's weapon (5)
Coach wanted Rusty-James to beat him up (3)
Coach who wanted Rusty-James to beat up a student (4)
Fat, but tough: B. J. ___ (7)
Guidance counselor (8)
It didn't scare Rusty-James (4)
It had a picture of Motorcycle Boy (8)
It ruined the gangs. (4)
It said a lot of bad words (6)
Junior high hangout: ____'s (5)
Knifed Rusty-James: ___ Wilcox (4)
Local gang (7)
Pee-wee branch of the local gang: ___ Leaguers (6)
Pet store owner (7)
Police officer who shot the Motorcycle Boy (9)
Rusty-James drank it a lot: ___ Pete (6)
Rusty-James drank it before a fight: chocolate ___ (4)
Rusty-James insulted her (5)
Rusty-James jumped from one to another (4)
Rusty-James liked the excitement there (4)
Rusty-James wanted to be like his ___ (7)
Rusty-James's best friend (5)

Rusty-James's father was an ex-____ who drank all day (6)
Rusty-James's girlfriend (5)
Rusty-James's only vice (7)
School Rusty-James did not want to attend (9)
She liked Steve but not Rusty-James: ___ Martin (7)
Siamese fighting fish that killed each other (10)
Steve didn't like the movies there: ___ City (3)
Steve's mother was there (8)
Student teacher who liked the Motorcycle Boy (9)
Tallest boy in the crowd (6)
The Motorcycle Boy broke into it: ___ store (3)
The Motorcycle Boy died from it (4)
The Motorcycle Boy took the ___ flying fish to the river (7)
The Motorcycle Boy went there (10)
The Motorcycle Boy's condition: color ___ (5)
The Motorcycle Boy's scared Rusty-James (5)
The car with mag wheels (5)
The hubcaps Rusty-James tried to steal (4)
Where the story started (5)
Would have been Biff's gang: ___ Hawks (5)
Would have been the top tough guy (6)
____ Boy didn't belong anywhere (10)

Rumble Fish Word Search 2

```
K N O S K C A J C A L I F O R N I A H K
N Z G P I L J W T H Y D G W K F K D N S
I D X V M A H P C B Y F J Q W M G O B B
F N K G P M M H H A R R I G A N F N R J
E A T G A M N E Q E P O D A R B M N O C
Z L C Z T M B C S K A B V N C R I E T R
R E T Q T S T L I E T B P I S Y D L H M
G V X H E O Y A J T T I E T X N G Y E X
R E F O R M A T O R Y F L A W Y E R R N
B L X R S M E I M K G F R D C N T A I H
L C A D O P D P I Q P D V Z I H S A K D
M P C O N D V S L C N E Y Z P S P X X Y
G O S N Y L X O K A I N A L I H M R K V
B Y T D H L N H S N N G W N W O B I D J
K P Q O J Q C S N E A X W C S T S N L L
R O O F R L A A B M W Y N H M T I Z L E
Y Z V S W C E F G Y A N X E T L E I W L
K V P Y B J Y F H T W G H V B Z V V J B
X L N X T K T C W R G Y S Y B E Q V E Z
P A C K E R S E L T T I L S D R Y A N C
C N S L X B M T T E B R S M O K E Y H J
C Z N L O Y A L T Y R U M B L E F I S H
```

Bill's weapon (5)
Coach wanted Rusty-James to beat him up (3)
Coach who wanted Rusty-James to beat up a student (4)
Fat, but tough: B. J. ___ (7)
Guidance counselor (8)
It didn't scare Rusty-James (4)
It had a picture of Motorcycle Boy (8)
It ruined the gangs. (4)
It said a lot of bad words (6)
Junior high hangout: ____'s (5)
Knifed Rusty-James: ___ Wilcox (4)
Local gang (7)
Pee-wee branch of the local gang: ___ Leaguers (6)
Pet store owner (7)
Police officer who shot the Motorcycle Boy (9)
Rusty-James drank it a lot: ___ Pete (6)
Rusty-James drank it before a fight: chocolate ___ (4)
Rusty-James insulted her (5)
Rusty-James jumped from one to another (4)
Rusty-James liked the excitement there (4)
Rusty-James spent five years there (11)
Rusty-James wanted to be like his ___ (7)
Rusty-James's best friend (5)

Rusty-James's father was an ex-____ who drank all day (6)
Rusty-James's girlfriend (5)
Rusty-James's only vice (7)
School Rusty-James did not want to attend (9)
She liked Steve but not Rusty-James: ___ Martin (7)
Siamese fighting fish that killed each other (10)
Steve didn't like the movies there: ___ City (3)
Steve's mother was there (8)
Student teacher who liked the Motorcycle Boy (9)
Tallest boy in the crowd (6)
The Motorcycle Boy broke into it: ___ store (3)
The Motorcycle Boy died from it (4)
The Motorcycle Boy took the ___ flying fish to the river (7)
The Motorcycle Boy went there (10)
The Motorcycle Boy's condition: color ___ (5)
The Motorcycle Boy's scared Rusty-James (5)
The car with mag wheels (5)
The hubcaps Rusty-James tried to steal (4)
Where the story started (5)
Would have been Biff's gang: ___ Hawks (5)
Would have been the top tough guy (6)
____ Boy didn't belong anywhere (10)

Rumble Fish Word Search 2 Answer Key

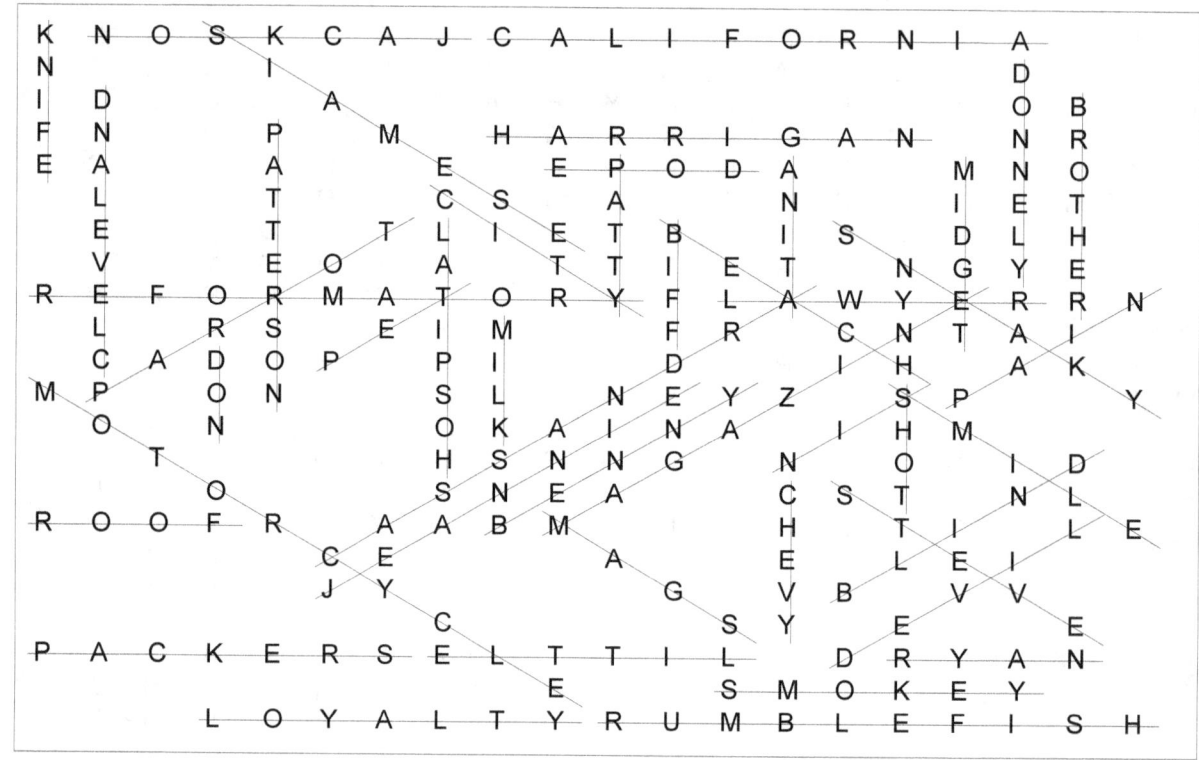

Bill's weapon (5)
Coach wanted Rusty-James to beat him up (3)
Coach who wanted Rusty-James to beat up a student (4)
Fat, but tough: B. J. ___ (7)
Guidance counselor (8)
It didn't scare Rusty-James (4)
It had a picture of Motorcycle Boy (8)
It ruined the gangs. (4)
It said a lot of bad words (6)
Junior high hangout: ____'s (5)
Knifed Rusty-James: ___ Wilcox (4)
Local gang (7)
Pee-wee branch of the local gang: ___ Leaguers (6)
Pet store owner (7)
Police officer who shot the Motorcycle Boy (9)
Rusty-James drank it a lot: ___ Pete (6)
Rusty-James drank it before a fight: chocolate ___ (4)
Rusty-James insulted her (5)
Rusty-James jumped from one to another (4)
Rusty-James liked the excitement there (4)
Rusty-James spent five years there (11)
Rusty-James wanted to be like his ___ (7)
Rusty-James's best friend (5)

Rusty-James's father was an ex-____ who drank all day (6)
Rusty-James's girlfriend (5)
Rusty-James's only vice (7)
School Rusty-James did not want to attend (9)
She liked Steve but not Rusty-James: ___ Martin (7)
Siamese fighting fish that killed each other (10)
Steve didn't like the movies there: ___ City (3)
Steve's mother was there (8)
Student teacher who liked the Motorcycle Boy (9)
Tallest boy in the crowd (6)
The Motorcycle Boy broke into it: ___ store (3)
The Motorcycle Boy died from it (4)
The Motorcycle Boy took the ___ flying fish to the river (7)
The Motorcycle Boy went there (10)
The Motorcycle Boy's condition: color ___ (5)
The Motorcycle Boy's scared Rusty-James (5)
The car with mag wheels (5)
The hubcaps Rusty-James tried to steal (4)
Where the story started (5)
Would have been Biff's gang: ___ Hawks (5)
Would have been the top tough guy (6)
____ Boy didn't belong anywhere (10)

Rumble Fish Word Search 3

```
D O N N E L Y C C A L I F O R N I A Y V
R C P H W F B Q L M H B M D Z R F E B W
E X A V W M P C E M T B P W W G K R M T
F F C W M W Y S V O M C N Z T O X R L C
O X K H C H B G E T J P R B M S M V V D
R R E O H M L P L O C B S S B A Q P G V
M P R S Q B O T A R J K G I G B K J Y C
A T S P W J Y N N C X Y F A A L Y J Q G
T Z P I S H A B D Y S C Z K F M R P D G
O Y Y T G H L T P C S I H N D P E Y O R
R J E A K X T N B L N P S O L Z T S P Z
Y V Q L A W Y E R E L I M S M I D G E T
E G I V F K T M I N N L G R C K F F T V
J M V M A O D N A Q N N R E K Y I D H M
A B B E R B N G H O H Y Y T Z N H C Z W
C K N R L A I V D L W Z A T K P A I N Z
K S A C E R L F I F B F N A P E A J C G
S P C J R B B V F J K C I P B K W T N M
O M P A O L E F Y Q H T D Q S F O T B
N G H F O D L I T T L E A K G C T H K Y
X H S I F E L B M U R V W A Q K B S T N
C A S S A N D R A Q N Y M B R O T H E R
```

ANITA	CITY	JEANNIE	MOTORCYCLE	RUMBLEFISH
BEACH	CLEVELAND	KNIFE	PACKERS	RYAN
BENNY	DEVIL	LAWYER	PAIN	SHOT
BIFF	DON	LITTLE	PARROT	SIAMESE
BLIND	DONNELY	LOYALTY	PATTERSON	SIN
BROTHER	DOPE	MAGAZINE	PATTY	SMILE
CALIFORNIA	HARRIGAN	MAGS	PET	SMOKEY
CASSANDRA	HOSPITAL	MIDGET	REFORMATORY	SNEAKY
CHEVY	JACKSON	MILK	ROOF	STEVE

Rumble Fish Word Search 3 Answer Key

```
D   O   N   N   E   L   Y       C   A   L   I   F   O   R   N   I   A   Y
R       P                       L               E                           K
E       A   C   K   E   R   S   M   O                   S   S       A   M   O
F       C           H                   T                   I       G       M
O       K           O           L   O   O               S   A   A   M
R       E           S   L       A   T                   Z   N           E   D
M       R           P   O       N   O       B               S   M   I   E   S   O
A       S           I   Y       D   R   E   I   L   I   M   S   C   D   G   T   P
T               E   T   A       B   C           R       N   R       T   G   F   E
O       V       L   A   W   Y   E   R   I   N   N       R       I   N   C   T
R   M           I   L                   N   G       N   Y   I   N   K       A   I   H
Y       N   S   A   K   E   R   B   A           D   O   L   D       P   E   A   N
E       J           E   R       A   I   L   F           N   I       A       S       T
J               P       J   A   R   O       V   C   H   I   T   B           O   T   Y
O                       H       A   O   D   L   I   T   T   L   E   V   T   T
N                       S   I   F   E   L   B   M   U   R       Y   M   B   R   O   T   H   E   R
C   A   S   S   A   N   D   R   A
```

ANITA	CITY	JEANNIE	MOTORCYCLE	RUMBLEFISH
BEACH	CLEVELAND	KNIFE	PACKERS	RYAN
BENNY	DEVIL	LAWYER	PAIN	SHOT
BIFF	DON	LITTLE	PARROT	SIAMESE
BLIND	DONNELY	LOYALTY	PATTERSON	SIN
BROTHER	DOPE	MAGAZINE	PATTY	SMILE
CALIFORNIA	HARRIGAN	MAGS	PET	SMOKEY
CASSANDRA	HOSPITAL	MIDGET	REFORMATORY	SNEAKY
CHEVY	JACKSON	MILK	ROOF	STEVE

Rumble Fish Word Search 4

```
D C A L I F O R N I A J E A N N I E H M
P O H Z S D L D L Q V A C N Y T X P J O X
A F P R M G O L S G D C I H Y F A M S Q
I P A E O W Y F V L H K Z M T V T O P Y
N B R V K L A W Y E R S A B A X T T I Z
P S R J E D L X V O E O G L E G Y O T P
S W O O Y W T Y O Y F N A I G N S R A R
N T T X T T Y F R Q O X M N C B N C L T
X S E X X H V Y Q U R X F D C Y E Y T M
Z J C V V M E X H T M J F B N Q A C H X
S I A M E S E R C F A B B N K K K L Q M
S Y S Q P N F J P Y T P L J B Z Y E F N
H X S C R D V J G R O G A E Q S W K L W
V F A Z W N B M F B R M B T F M N Y V N
G H N T Y A K F C S Y C F S T I S S Y F
B P D N J L Z R G D R F S R F E S L T G
F P R Z T E Y H E Z S E H E H H R H W R
X S A B N V J D H L Y R K Z C F S E Y A
X H W X X E I T C T M V J C Q C F L O A
D O N N E L Y A T I N A H A R R I G A N
V T K Q J C E I L D J R S P B M B T L G
S I N O D B L K M I D G E T S P E T Y S
```

ANITA	CITY	JEANNIE	MOTORCYCLE	RUMBLEFISH
BEACH	CLEVELAND	KNIFE	PACKERS	RYAN
BENNY	DEVIL	LAWYER	PAIN	SHOT
BIFF	DON	LITTLE	PARROT	SIAMESE
BLIND	DONNELY	LOYALTY	PATTERSON	SIN
BROTHER	DOPE	MAGAZINE	PATTY	SMILE
CALIFORNIA	HARRIGAN	MAGS	PET	SMOKEY
CASSANDRA	HOSPITAL	MIDGET	REFORMATORY	SNEAKY
CHEVY	JACKSON	MILK	ROOF	STEVE

Rumble Fish Word Search 4 Answer Key

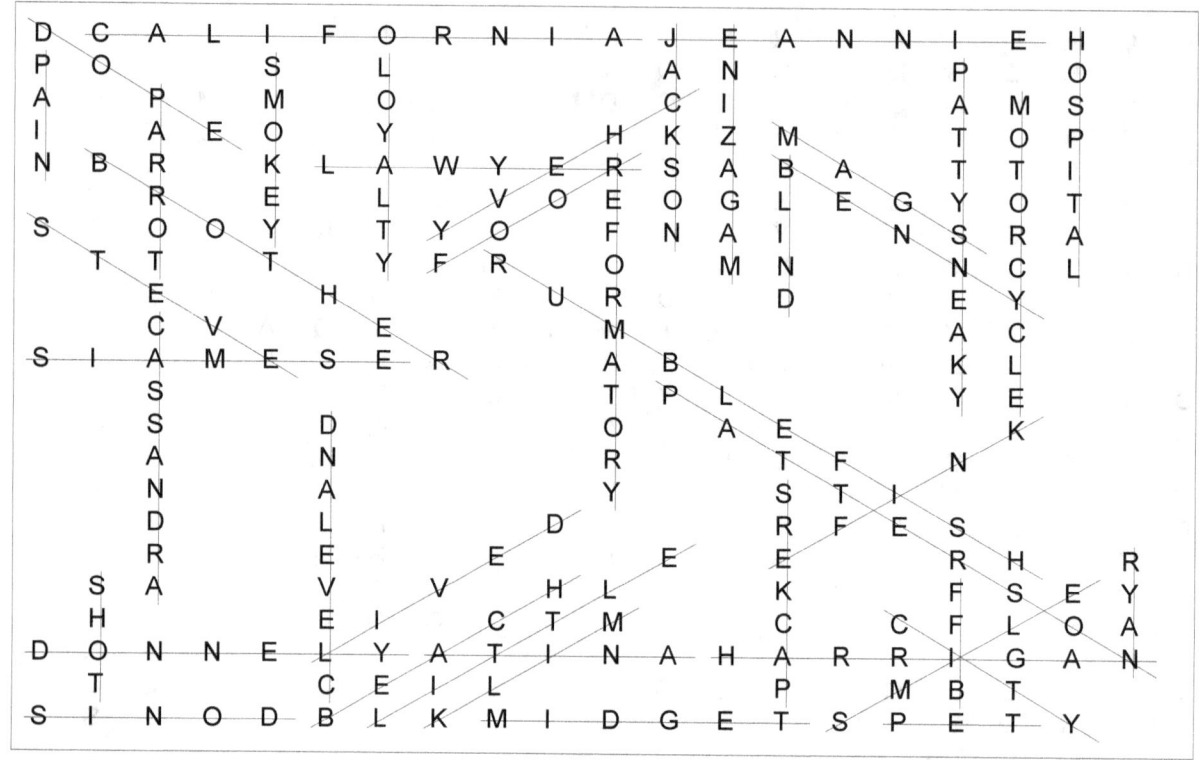

ANITA	CITY	JEANNIE	MOTORCYCLE	RUMBLEFISH
BEACH	CLEVELAND	KNIFE	PACKERS	RYAN
BENNY	DEVIL	LAWYER	PAIN	SHOT
BIFF	DON	LITTLE	PARROT	SIAMESE
BLIND	DONNELY	LOYALTY	PATTERSON	SIN
BROTHER	DOPE	MAGAZINE	PATTY	SMILE
CALIFORNIA	HARRIGAN	MAGS	PET	SMOKEY
CASSANDRA	HOSPITAL	MIDGET	REFORMATORY	SNEAKY
CHEVY	JACKSON	MILK	ROOF	STEVE

Rumble Fish Crossword 1

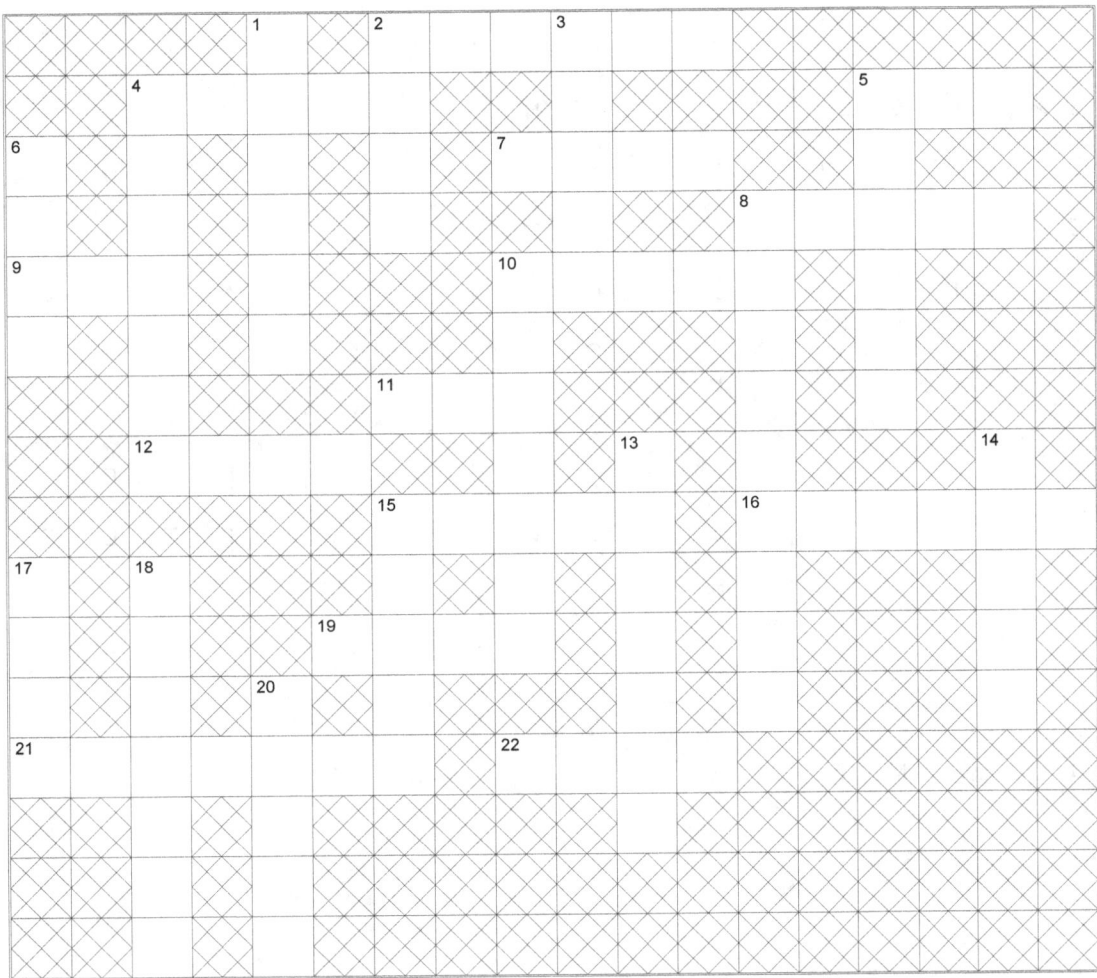

Across
2. Would have been the top tough guy
4. Where the story started
5. Steve didn't like the movies there: ___ City
7. Rusty-James drank it before a fight: chocolate ___
8. The car with mag wheels
9. The Motorcycle Boy broke into it: ___ store
10. Would have been Biff's gang: ___ Hawks
11. Coach wanted Rusty-James to beat him up
12. Rusty-James jumped from one to another
15. Rusty-James's best friend
16. Pee-wee branch of the local gang: ___ Leaguers
19. Rusty-James liked the excitement there
21. The Motorcycle Boy took the ___ flying fish to the river
22. It didn't scare Rusty-James

Down
1. Rusty-James's father was an ex-___ who drank all day
2. The Motorcycle Boy died from it
3. Bill's weapon
4. Rusty-James wanted to be like his ___
5. Rusty-James drank it a lot: ___ Pete
6. It ruined the gangs.
8. School Rusty-James did not want to attend
10. Pet store owner
13. She liked Steve but not Rusty-James: ___ Martin
14. The Motorcycle Boy's condition: color ___
15. The Motorcycle Boy's scared Rusty-James
17. The hubcaps Rusty-James tried to steal
18. Rusty-James's only vice
20. Junior high hangout: ____'s

Rumble Fish Crossword 1 Answer Key

					1 L	2 S	M	3 O	K	E	Y				
		4 B	E	A	C	H		N					5 S	I	N
6 D		R		W		O		7 M	I	L	K		N		
O		O		Y		T		I				8 C	H	E	V	Y
9 P	E	T		E				10 D	E	V	I	L		A	
E		H		R				O				E		K	
		E				11 D	O	N				V		Y	
		12 R	O	O	F			N		13 J		E			14 B
						15 S	T	E	V	E		16 L	I	T	T	L	E
17 M		18 L						M		L		A			I
A		O		19 C	I	T	Y			A		N			N
G		Y		20 B		L				N		D			D
21 S	I	A	M	E	S	E		22 P	A	I	N				
		L		N						E					
		T		N											
		Y		Y											

Across
2. Would have been the top tough guy
4. Where the story started
5. Steve didn't like the movies there: ___ City
7. Rusty-James drank it before a fight: chocolate ___
8. The car with mag wheels
9. The Motorcycle Boy broke into it: ___ store
10. Would have been Biff's gang: ___ Hawks
11. Coach wanted Rusty-James to beat him up
12. Rusty-James jumped from one to another
15. Rusty-James's best friend
16. Pee-wee branch of the local gang: ___ Leaguers
19. Rusty-James liked the excitement there
21. The Motorcycle Boy took the ___ flying fish to the river
22. It didn't scare Rusty-James

Down
1. Rusty-James's father was an ex-____ who drank all day
2. The Motorcycle Boy died from it
3. Bill's weapon
4. Rusty-James wanted to be like his ___
5. Rusty-James drank it a lot: ___ Pete
6. It ruined the gangs.
8. School Rusty-James did not want to attend
10. Pet store owner
13. She liked Steve but not Rusty-James: ___ Martin
14. The Motorcycle Boy's condition: color ___
15. The Motorcycle Boy's scared Rusty-James
17. The hubcaps Rusty-James tried to steal
18. Rusty-James's only vice
20. Junior high hangout: ____'s

Rumble Fish Crossword 2

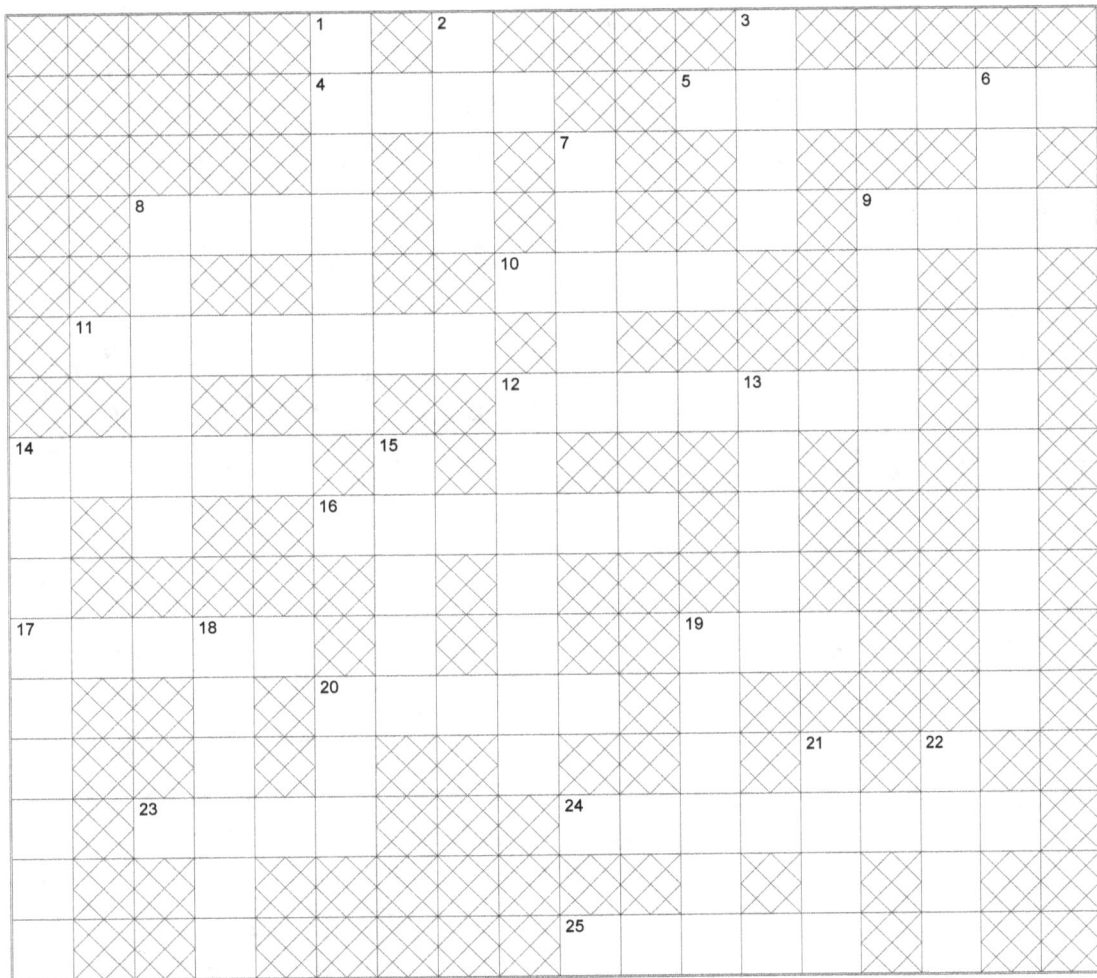

Across
4. Rusty-James jumped from one to another
5. Local gang
8. The Motorcycle Boy died from it
9. Knifed Rusty-James: ___ Wilcox
10. Rusty-James drank it before a fight: chocolate ___
11. Pet store owner
12. Fat, but tough: B. J. ___
14. The car with mag wheels
16. Rusty-James drank it a lot: ___ Pete
17. The Motorcycle Boy's scared Rusty-James
19. The Motorcycle Boy broke into it: ___ store
20. Would have been Biff's gang: ___ Hawks
23. Coach who wanted Rusty-James to beat up a student
24. Guidance counselor
25. Rusty-James's girlfriend

Down
1. Rusty-James wanted to be like his ___
2. It ruined the gangs.
3. The hubcaps Rusty-James tried to steal
6. Rusty-James spent five years there
7. Rusty-James insulted her
8. Would have been the top tough guy
9. The Motorcycle Boy's condition: color ___
12. She liked Steve but not Rusty-James: ___ Martin
13. Rusty-James's best friend
14. Student teacher who liked the Motorcycle Boy
15. Bill's weapon
18. Rusty-James's father was an ex-____ who drank all day
19. It said a lot of bad words
20. Coach wanted Rusty-James to beat him up
21. Rusty-James liked the excitement there
22. It didn't scare Rusty-James

Rumble Fish Crossword 2 Answer Key

			1 B	2 D			3 M		
		4 R	O	O	F	5 P	A	C	K	E	R	S
		O		P		7 A		G			E	
	8 S	H	O	T		E		N		S		9 B	I	F	F
	M		H		10 M	I	L	K		L		O
11 D	O	N	N	E	L	Y		T			I		R
	K		R			12 J	A	C	K	13 S	O	N		M
14 C	H	E	V	Y		15 K		E			T		D		A
A		Y			16 S	N	E	A	K	Y		E			T
S					I			N			V			O
17 S	M	18 I	L	E		F		N		19 P	E	T			R
A		L			20 D	E	V	I	L		A			Y
N		A			O			E		R		21 C		22 P
D		23 R	Y	A	N			24 H	A	R	R	I	G	A	N
R		E								O		T		I
A		R			25 P	A	T	T	Y			N

Across

4. Rusty-James jumped from one to another
5. Local gang
8. The Motorcycle Boy died from it
9. Knifed Rusty-James: ___ Wilcox
10. Rusty-James drank it before a fight: chocolate ___
11. Pet store owner
12. Fat, but tough: B. J. ___
14. The car with mag wheels
16. Rusty-James drank it a lot: ___ Pete
17. The Motorcycle Boy's scared Rusty-James
19. The Motorcycle Boy broke into it: ___ store
20. Would have been Biff's gang: ___ Hawks
23. Coach who wanted Rusty-James to beat up a student
24. Guidance counselor
25. Rusty-James's girlfriend

Down

1. Rusty-James wanted to be like his ___
2. It ruined the gangs.
3. The hubcaps Rusty-James tried to steal
6. Rusty-James spent five years there
7. Rusty-James insulted her
8. Would have been the top tough guy
9. The Motorcycle Boy's condition: color ___
12. She liked Steve but not Rusty-James: ___ Martin
13. Rusty-James's best friend
14. Student teacher who liked the Motorcycle Boy
15. Bill's weapon
18. Rusty-James's father was an ex-____ who drank all day
19. It said a lot of bad words
20. Coach wanted Rusty-James to beat him up
21. Rusty-James liked the excitement there
22. It didn't scare Rusty-James

Rumble Fish Crossword 3

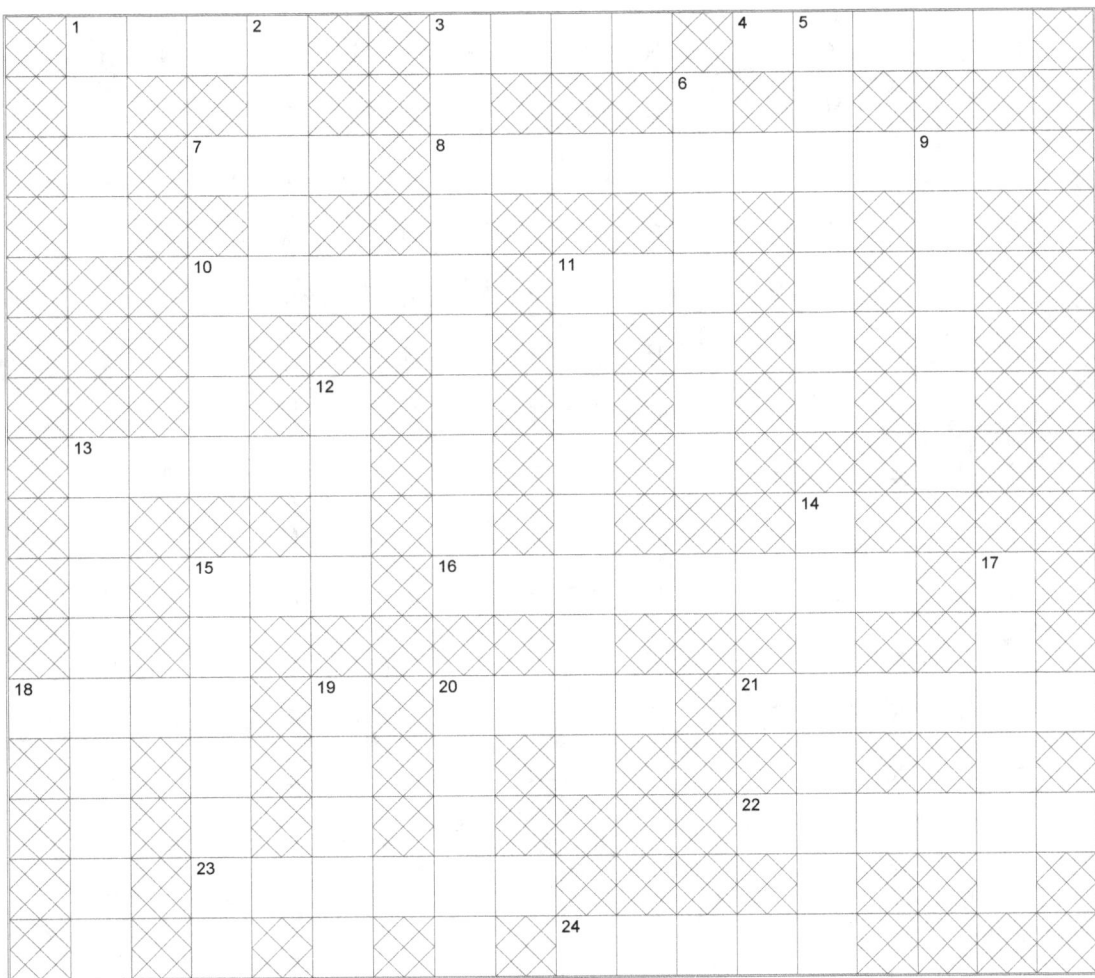

Across
1. Rusty-James drank it before a fight: chocolate ___
3. Rusty-James jumped from one to another
4. The Motorcycle Boy's condition: color ___
7. Steve didn't like the movies there: ___ City
8. ___ Boy didn't belong anywhere
10. Would have been Biff's gang: ___ Hawks
11. The Motorcycle Boy broke into it: ___ store
13. The car with mag wheels
15. Coach wanted Rusty-James to beat him up
16. Guidance counselor
18. It didn't scare Rusty-James
20. The Motorcycle Boy died from it
21. It said a lot of bad words
22. Tallest boy in the crowd
23. Pee-wee branch of the local gang: ___ Leaguers
24. Rusty-James's best friend

Down
1. The hubcaps Rusty-James tried to steal
2. Bill's weapon
3. Siamese fighting fish that killed each other
5. Rusty-James's only vice
6. Rusty-James wanted to be like his ___
9. Rusty-James's father was an ex-____ who drank all day
10. It ruined the gangs.
11. Police officer who shot the Motorcycle Boy
12. Coach who wanted Rusty-James to beat up a student
13. Student teacher who liked the Motorcycle Boy
14. It had a picture of Motorcycle Boy
15. Pet store owner
17. Would have been the top tough guy
19. Rusty-James's girlfriend
20. The Motorcycle Boy's scared Rusty-James

Rumble Fish Crossword 3 Answer Key

	1 M	I	L	2 K		3 R	O	O	F		4 B	5 L	I	N	D
	A			N		U				6 B		O			
	G		7 S	I	N	8 M	O	T	O	R	C	Y	9 C	L	E
	S			F		B				O		A		A	
			10 D	E	V	I	L		11 P	E	T		L		W
			O			E			A		H		T		Y
			P		12 R	F			T		E		Y		E
	13 C	H	E	V	Y		I		T		R				R
	A				A		S		E				14 M		
	S		15 D	O	N		16 H	A	R	R	I	G	A	N	17 S
	S		O				S						G		M
18 P	A	I	N		19 P	20 S	H	O	T		21 P	A	R	R	O	T
	N		N		A		M		N			Z			K	
	D		E		A	T		I				22 M	I	D	G	E	T
	R		23 L	I	T	T	L	E				N			Y	
	A		Y		Y		E		24 S	T	E	V	E			

Across
1. Rusty-James drank it before a fight: chocolate ___
3. Rusty-James jumped from one to another
4. The Motorcycle Boy's condition: color ___
7. Steve didn't like the movies there: ___ City
8. ____ Boy didn't belong anywhere
10. Would have been Biff's gang: ___ Hawks
11. The Motorcycle Boy broke into it: ___ store
13. The car with mag wheels
15. Coach wanted Rusty-James to beat him up
16. Guidance counselor
18. It didn't scare Rusty-James
20. The Motorcycle Boy died from it
21. It said a lot of bad words
22. Tallest boy in the crowd
23. Pee-wee branch of the local gang: ___ Leaguers
24. Rusty-James's best friend

Down
1. The hubcaps Rusty-James tried to steal
2. Bill's weapon
3. Siamese fighting fish that killed each other
5. Rusty-James's only vice
6. Rusty-James wanted to be like his ___
9. Rusty-James's father was an ex-____ who drank all day
10. It ruined the gangs.
11. Police officer who shot the Motorcycle Boy
12. Coach who wanted Rusty-James to beat up a student
13. Student teacher who liked the Motorcycle Boy
14. It had a picture of Motorcycle Boy
15. Pet store owner
17. Would have been the top tough guy
19. Rusty-James's girlfriend
20. The Motorcycle Boy's scared Rusty-James

Rumble Fish Crossword 4

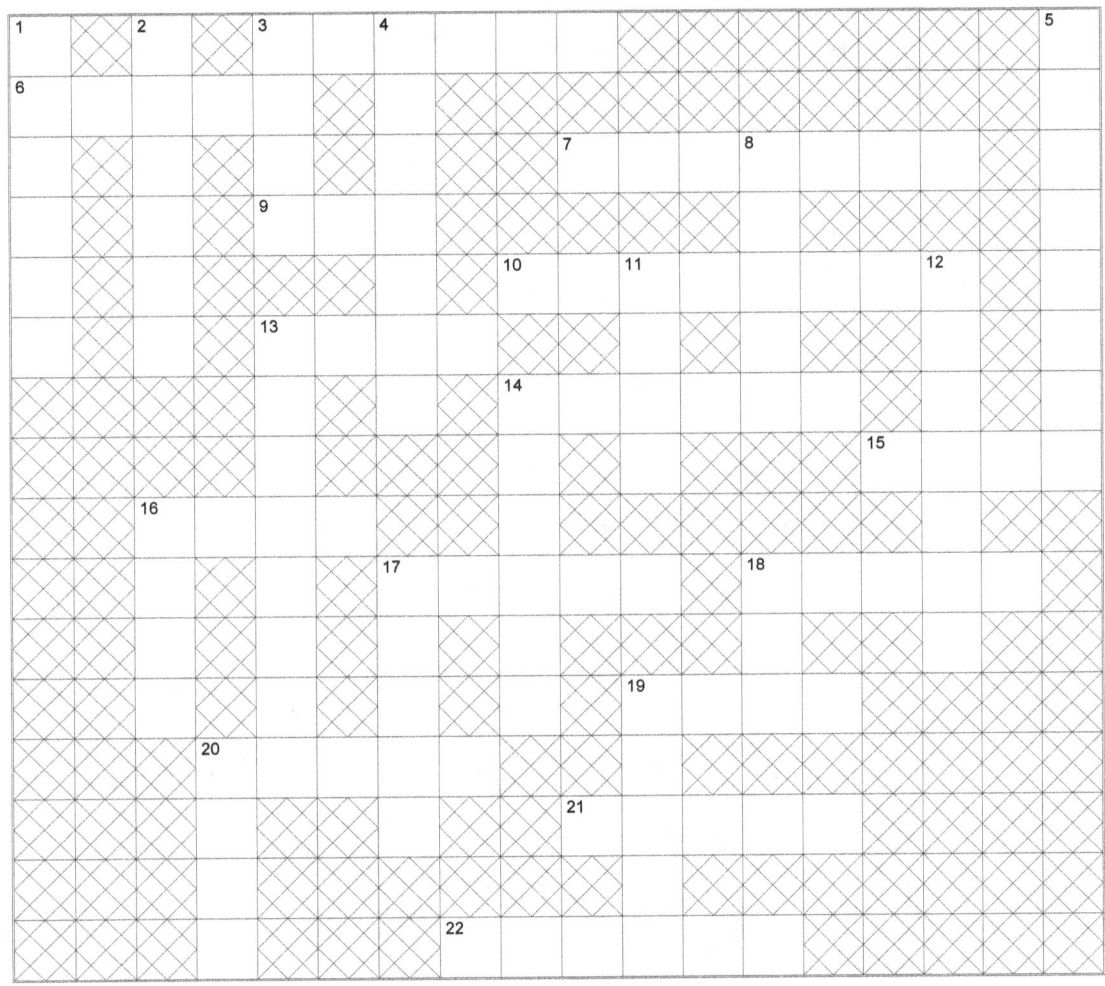

Across
3. Tallest boy in the crowd
6. Rusty-James insulted her
7. Local gang
9. Steve didn't like the movies there: ___ City
10. Steve's mother was there
13. Rusty-James drank it before a fight: chocolate ___
14. Would have been the top tough guy
15. It didn't scare Rusty-James
16. Coach who wanted Rusty-James to beat up a student
17. Where the story started
18. Rusty-James's girlfriend
19. Rusty-James liked the excitement there
20. Junior high hangout: ____'s
21. Would have been Biff's gang: ___ Hawks
22. Rusty-James's father was an ex-____ who drank all day

Down
1. It said a lot of bad words
2. Pee-wee branch of the local gang: ___ Leaguers
3. The hubcaps Rusty-James tried to steal
4. Pet store owner
5. Guidance counselor
8. Bill's weapon
11. The Motorcycle Boy died from it
12. Rusty-James's only vice
13. It had a picture of Motorcycle Boy
14. Rusty-James drank it a lot: ___ Pete
16. Rusty-James jumped from one to another
17. The Motorcycle Boy's condition: color ___
18. The Motorcycle Boy broke into it: ___ store
19. The car with mag wheels
20. Knifed Rusty-James: ___ Wilcox

Rumble Fish Crossword 4 Answer Key

	1 P		2 L		3 M	I	4 D	G	E	T						5 H
	6 A	N	I	T	A		O									A
	R		T		G		N			7 P	A	C	8 K	E	R	S	R
	R		T		9 S	I	N						N			R
	O		L				E		10 H	O	11 S	P	I	T	A	12 L	I
	T		E		13 M	I	L	K		H		F			O	G
					A		Y		14 S	M	O	K	E	Y		Y	A
					G				N		T				15 P	A	I	N
			16 R	Y	A	N			E						L
			O		Z		17 B	E	A	C	H		18 P	A	T	T	Y
			O		I		L		K				E			Y
			F		N		I		Y		19 C	I	T	Y
				20 B	E	N	N	Y		H
				I			D		21 D	E	V	I	L
				F					V
				F			22 L	A	W	Y	E	R

Across
3. Tallest boy in the crowd
6. Rusty-James insulted her
7. Local gang
9. Steve didn't like the movies there: ___ City
10. Steve's mother was there
13. Rusty-James drank it before a fight: chocolate ___
14. Would have been the top tough guy
15. It didn't scare Rusty-James
16. Coach who wanted Rusty-James to beat up a student
17. Where the story started
18. Rusty-James's girlfriend
19. Rusty-James liked the excitement there
20. Junior high hangout: ____'s
21. Would have been Biff's gang: ___ Hawks
22. Rusty-James's father was an ex-____ who drank all day

Down
1. It said a lot of bad words
2. Pee-wee branch of the local gang: ___ Leaguers
3. The hubcaps Rusty-James tried to steal
4. Pet store owner
5. Guidance counselor
8. Bill's weapon
11. The Motorcycle Boy died from it
12. Rusty-James's only vice
13. It had a picture of Motorcycle Boy
14. Rusty-James drank it a lot: ___ Pete
16. Rusty-James jumped from one to another
17. The Motorcycle Boy's condition: color ___
18. The Motorcycle Boy broke into it: ___ store
19. The car with mag wheels
20. Knifed Rusty-James: ___ Wilcox

Rumble Fish

MIDGET	CALIFORNIA	ROOF	PACKERS	DONNELY
REFORMATORY	PARROT	CASSANDRA	LITTLE	SIN
DON	CLEVELAND	FREE SPACE	BROTHER	PAIN
MAGS	JACKSON	RUMBLEFISH	STEVE	SHOT
LAWYER	JEANNIE	MILK	PATTY	BEACH

Rumble Fish

SMILE	RYAN	DEVIL	SNEAKY	BENNY
ANITA	PATTERSON	PET	MOTORCYCLE	CITY
BIFF	MAGAZINE	FREE SPACE	SIAMESE	HOSPITAL
HARRIGAN	BLIND	DOPE	KNIFE	SMOKEY
BEACH	PATTY	MILK	JEANNIE	LAWYER

Rumble Fish

RYAN	CASSANDRA	RUMBLEFISH	PET	SIN
LITTLE	BENNY	BROTHER	BLIND	SNEAKY
PACKERS	DOPE	FREE SPACE	JEANNIE	PATTERSON
SHOT	MIDGET	DONNELY	SMILE	MAGS
LAWYER	KNIFE	DEVIL	PAIN	JACKSON

Rumble Fish

STEVE	CHEVY	CITY	HARRIGAN	PATTY
ANITA	HOSPITAL	CLEVELAND	MILK	LOYALTY
SMOKEY	BIFF	FREE SPACE	DON	SIAMESE
CALIFORNIA	MAGAZINE	ROOF	MOTORCYCLE	PARROT
JACKSON	PAIN	DEVIL	KNIFE	LAWYER

Rumble Fish

ANITA	SHOT	CHEVY	DEVIL	ROOF
MOTORCYCLE	PATTERSON	SMILE	MAGAZINE	PATTY
MAGS	JEANNIE	FREE SPACE	CLEVELAND	REFORMATORY
KNIFE	SNEAKY	PACKERS	DON	PARROT
SIN	DONNELY	BENNY	DOPE	HOSPITAL

Rumble Fish

BLIND	RYAN	STEVE	HARRIGAN	LOYALTY
BIFF	PAIN	CALIFORNIA	MILK	BROTHER
JACKSON	MIDGET	FREE SPACE	CITY	BEACH
SMOKEY	SIAMESE	PET	RUMBLEFISH	CASSANDRA
HOSPITAL	DOPE	BENNY	DONNELY	SIN

Rumble Fish

MIDGET	CALIFORNIA	LAWYER	MOTORCYCLE	CLEVELAND
LITTLE	ANITA	DEVIL	JEANNIE	RYAN
SHOT	MAGAZINE	FREE SPACE	HOSPITAL	DONNELY
BENNY	MAGS	HARRIGAN	PAIN	PATTY
CHEVY	RUMBLEFISH	DON	SMOKEY	MILK

Rumble Fish

ROOF	SIN	BEACH	DOPE	STEVE
SNEAKY	CASSANDRA	BROTHER	CITY	BIFF
KNIFE	PARROT	FREE SPACE	JACKSON	PATTERSON
REFORMATORY	LOYALTY	PACKERS	SMILE	BLIND
MILK	SMOKEY	DON	RUMBLEFISH	CHEVY

48
Copyrighted

Rumble Fish

DONNELY	CALIFORNIA	BLIND	LOYALTY	PACKERS
DEVIL	REFORMATORY	BENNY	JEANNIE	CASSANDRA
CLEVELAND	DOPE	FREE SPACE	MOTORCYCLE	MAGS
SIAMESE	CITY	LAWYER	SHOT	STEVE
ROOF	DON	BIFF	MAGAZINE	ANITA

Rumble Fish

RYAN	KNIFE	PATTERSON	MILK	BROTHER
SMOKEY	PATTY	SMILE	BEACH	PARROT
SIN	MIDGET	FREE SPACE	PAIN	HOSPITAL
PET	RUMBLEFISH	JACKSON	HARRIGAN	SNEAKY
ANITA	MAGAZINE	BIFF	DON	ROOF

Rumble Fish

JACKSON	ANITA	HARRIGAN	BLIND	RUMBLEFISH
PET	STEVE	MOTORCYCLE	PATTERSON	MAGS
CITY	LOYALTY	FREE SPACE	PATTY	REFORMATORY
SHOT	DEVIL	RYAN	PAIN	PACKERS
MAGAZINE	CHEVY	SIN	SNEAKY	HOSPITAL

Rumble Fish

ROOF	SIAMESE	CLEVELAND	MILK	JEANNIE
BEACH	BENNY	DOPE	KNIFE	BIFF
BROTHER	PARROT	FREE SPACE	MIDGET	SMILE
LITTLE	CALIFORNIA	CASSANDRA	DON	SMOKEY
HOSPITAL	SNEAKY	SIN	CHEVY	MAGAZINE

Rumble Fish

PARROT	CITY	SMILE	JACKSON	LAWYER
DOPE	MOTORCYCLE	SMOKEY	CALIFORNIA	RYAN
LITTLE	DON	FREE SPACE	LOYALTY	PACKERS
RUMBLEFISH	HARRIGAN	CASSANDRA	MAGS	REFORMATORY
DEVIL	JEANNIE	BIFF	STEVE	BENNY

Rumble Fish

SIAMESE	MAGAZINE	DONNELY	PATTERSON	SNEAKY
PET	ROOF	KNIFE	CHEVY	BROTHER
CLEVELAND	MIDGET	FREE SPACE	ANITA	BLIND
PAIN	HOSPITAL	MILK	BEACH	SHOT
BENNY	STEVE	BIFF	JEANNIE	DEVIL

Rumble Fish

DON	CALIFORNIA	RYAN	MOTORCYCLE	PACKERS
HOSPITAL	SHOT	MIDGET	CASSANDRA	SMILE
MAGS	PET	FREE SPACE	DONNELY	PARROT
SNEAKY	KNIFE	LAWYER	CHEVY	LOYALTY
CLEVELAND	MILK	BROTHER	ROOF	PAIN

Rumble Fish

DOPE	MAGAZINE	LITTLE	RUMBLEFISH	SMOKEY
JEANNIE	JACKSON	PATTY	BEACH	SIN
BENNY	CITY	FREE SPACE	PATTERSON	STEVE
REFORMATORY	HARRIGAN	DEVIL	BIFF	ANITA
PAIN	ROOF	BROTHER	MILK	CLEVELAND

Rumble Fish

MOTORCYCLE	BIFF	MIDGET	MAGAZINE	JACKSON
PATTERSON	PET	ROOF	HOSPITAL	LAWYER
PARROT	CHEVY	FREE SPACE	MAGS	KNIFE
BROTHER	SIAMESE	CLEVELAND	PACKERS	DONNELY
BLIND	PATTY	SMILE	SNEAKY	CASSANDRA

Rumble Fish

SMOKEY	STEVE	RYAN	MILK	BEACH
DEVIL	PAIN	REFORMATORY	SHOT	LOYALTY
ANITA	JEANNIE	FREE SPACE	SIN	CALIFORNIA
DOPE	BENNY	CITY	DON	HARRIGAN
CASSANDRA	SNEAKY	SMILE	PATTY	BLIND

Rumble Fish

LITTLE	MAGS	HARRIGAN	BEACH	CLEVELAND
DONNELY	SIAMESE	DEVIL	CALIFORNIA	RYAN
BLIND	SMILE	FREE SPACE	MIDGET	BROTHER
JACKSON	PAIN	JEANNIE	CITY	PATTERSON
RUMBLEFISH	KNIFE	MAGAZINE	PACKERS	PATTY

Rumble Fish

LAWYER	CHEVY	ANITA	REFORMATORY	SHOT
SMOKEY	STEVE	DON	SNEAKY	BIFF
ROOF	PET	FREE SPACE	PARROT	MOTORCYCLE
HOSPITAL	LOYALTY	DOPE	SIN	CASSANDRA
PATTY	PACKERS	MAGAZINE	KNIFE	RUMBLEFISH

Rumble Fish

SIN	LITTLE	SMILE	MAGAZINE	MOTORCYCLE
JACKSON	HOSPITAL	PACKERS	SIAMESE	PAIN
PATTERSON	PET	FREE SPACE	DONNELY	MAGS
CALIFORNIA	BLIND	DON	JEANNIE	PARROT
LAWYER	CITY	BIFF	CLEVELAND	ANITA

Rumble Fish

RYAN	BEACH	BENNY	STEVE	BROTHER
REFORMATORY	CASSANDRA	LOYALTY	CHEVY	DOPE
DEVIL	SMOKEY	FREE SPACE	MILK	SNEAKY
HARRIGAN	MIDGET	ROOF	PATTY	RUMBLEFISH
ANITA	CLEVELAND	BIFF	CITY	LAWYER

Rumble Fish

DONNELY	PATTY	SNEAKY	SIAMESE	SMOKEY
RUMBLEFISH	BENNY	CLEVELAND	CALIFORNIA	LITTLE
CASSANDRA	MIDGET	FREE SPACE	LOYALTY	HOSPITAL
PACKERS	HARRIGAN	SHOT	DEVIL	BIFF
KNIFE	JEANNIE	MAGAZINE	BROTHER	PAIN

Rumble Fish

CHEVY	DOPE	RYAN	BLIND	MAGS
BEACH	MILK	PATTERSON	JACKSON	ANITA
SIN	PARROT	FREE SPACE	CITY	STEVE
LAWYER	REFORMATORY	MOTORCYCLE	DON	PET
PAIN	BROTHER	MAGAZINE	JEANNIE	KNIFE

Rumble Fish

SIAMESE	DEVIL	MIDGET	SNEAKY	RUMBLEFISH
BIFF	BROTHER	KNIFE	PAIN	LITTLE
DON	STEVE	FREE SPACE	DOPE	LAWYER
REFORMATORY	PACKERS	SMILE	SHOT	BENNY
RYAN	ROOF	SIN	JEANNIE	PET

Rumble Fish

BEACH	SMOKEY	PATTY	CITY	MOTORCYCLE
ANITA	CALIFORNIA	PATTERSON	CASSANDRA	MILK
MAGS	HARRIGAN	FREE SPACE	HOSPITAL	PARROT
DONNELY	MAGAZINE	JACKSON	CLEVELAND	CHEVY
PET	JEANNIE	SIN	ROOF	RYAN

Rumble Fish

PARROT	CASSANDRA	LAWYER	ROOF	MAGAZINE
RYAN	MAGS	JEANNIE	HARRIGAN	SMOKEY
HOSPITAL	ANITA	FREE SPACE	CHEVY	CALIFORNIA
CITY	PATTERSON	SMILE	CLEVELAND	SIN
BLIND	PET	SIAMESE	SNEAKY	PAIN

Rumble Fish

DON	BENNY	PATTY	REFORMATORY	LITTLE
BROTHER	KNIFE	MOTORCYCLE	BEACH	BIFF
SHOT	DOPE	FREE SPACE	JACKSON	MILK
PACKERS	MIDGET	LOYALTY	DEVIL	RUMBLEFISH
PAIN	SNEAKY	SIAMESE	PET	BLIND

Rumble Fish

BIFF	ANITA	ROOF	MIDGET	SNEAKY
SMILE	SIAMESE	STEVE	LAWYER	SIN
LITTLE	BROTHER	FREE SPACE	DEVIL	BEACH
SHOT	CASSANDRA	DOPE	PAIN	PARROT
MAGS	CHEVY	DONNELY	PET	RYAN

Rumble Fish

KNIFE	DON	BLIND	LOYALTY	PACKERS
SMOKEY	CITY	MAGAZINE	CALIFORNIA	REFORMATORY
HARRIGAN	HOSPITAL	FREE SPACE	CLEVELAND	JACKSON
MILK	PATTY	PATTERSON	JEANNIE	MOTORCYCLE
RYAN	PET	DONNELY	CHEVY	MAGS

Rumble Fish

HOSPITAL	CHEVY	PET	BEACH	CALIFORNIA
CITY	MILK	SHOT	MOTORCYCLE	CLEVELAND
MAGAZINE	SIN	FREE SPACE	LOYALTY	LAWYER
DOPE	PATTERSON	PAIN	DONNELY	STEVE
KNIFE	CASSANDRA	DON	MIDGET	RUMBLEFISH

Rumble Fish

BROTHER	PACKERS	ANITA	MAGS	SMOKEY
SNEAKY	HARRIGAN	LITTLE	SIAMESE	ROOF
PATTY	PARROT	FREE SPACE	JEANNIE	SMILE
BLIND	REFORMATORY	BIFF	DEVIL	RYAN
RUMBLEFISH	MIDGET	DON	CASSANDRA	KNIFE

Rumble Fish Vocabulary Word List

No.	Word	Clue/Definition
1.	ABANDONED	Deserted; left
2.	ACUTE	Intense
3.	ALLIES	Supporters; partners
4.	ALTERNATIVE	Choice
5.	ATHEIST	One who does not believe in God
6.	CAUTIOUS	Careful
7.	CLIPPED	Hit with a sharp blow
8.	COMPLICATED	Difficult; involved
9.	CONTRARY	Opposite
10.	DAZEDLY	In a confused manner
11.	DISTORTED	Deformed; twisted out of shape
12.	DOZING	Napping
13.	ERA	A period of time
14.	EVENTUALLY	Finally
15.	INNATE	Inherited; inborn
16.	MANIAC	Madman; lunatic
17.	MISCAST	Put in an unsuitable role
18.	NOVELTY	New and unusual thing
19.	OBNOXIOUS	Offensive; annoying
20.	PAGAN	Person who worships many gods
21.	PERCEPTION	Insight
22.	PESTERED	Bothered; annoyed
23.	PRECEDENT	Example for future actions
24.	PRIMITIVE	Uncivilized; simple
25.	RASPING	Harsh, grating sound
26.	SARCASTIC	Mocking
27.	SASSY	Lively
28.	SCOWLING	Looking angry by lowering the eyebrows
29.	SCROUNGING	Searching
30.	SIMULATED	Imitation
31.	SOLITARY	Alone; single
32.	STALKING	Walking in an angry manner
33.	SUPERELITE	High-fashion
34.	TENSION	Anxiety; unease
35.	THROBBING	Aching
36.	TINGE	Small amount of color
37.	TOLERATE	Permit; endure
38.	VACANT	Empty

Rumble Fish Vocabulary Fill In The Blanks 1

_____ 1. Difficult; involved

_____ 2. Opposite

_____ 3. Searching

_____ 4. Napping

_____ 5. Example for future actions

_____ 6. Deserted; left

_____ 7. New and unusual thing

_____ 8. Walking in an angry manner

_____ 9. Empty

_____ 10. Uncivilized; simple

_____ 11. Alone; single

_____ 12. Looking angry by lowering the eyebrows

_____ 13. Offensive; annoying

_____ 14. Aching

_____ 15. High-fashion

_____ 16. Person who worships many gods

_____ 17. Harsh, grating sound

_____ 18. Permit; endure

_____ 19. Intense

_____ 20. Put in an unsuitable role

Rumble Fish Vocabulary Fill In The Blanks 1 Answer Key

COMPLICATED	1. Difficult; involved
CONTRARY	2. Opposite
SCROUNGING	3. Searching
DOZING	4. Napping
PRECEDENT	5. Example for future actions
ABANDONED	6. Deserted; left
NOVELTY	7. New and unusual thing
STALKING	8. Walking in an angry manner
VACANT	9. Empty
PRIMITIVE	10. Uncivilized; simple
SOLITARY	11. Alone; single
SCOWLING	12. Looking angry by lowering the eyebrows
OBNOXIOUS	13. Offensive; annoying
THROBBING	14. Aching
SUPERELITE	15. High-fashion
PAGAN	16. Person who worships many gods
RASPING	17. Harsh, grating sound
TOLERATE	18. Permit; endure
ACUTE	19. Intense
MISCAST	20. Put in an unsuitable role

Rumble Fish Vocabulary Fill In The Blanks 2

_____   1. Supporters; partners

_____   2. Small amount of color

_____   3. Harsh, grating sound

_____   4. Finally

_____   5. Lively

_____   6. One who does not believe in God

_____   7. Looking angry by lowering the eyebrows

_____   8. Searching

_____   9. Offensive; annoying

_____   10. Walking in an angry manner

_____   11. In a confused manner

_____   12. Deserted; left

_____   13. Insight

_____   14. Opposite

_____   15. Careful

_____   16. Inherited; inborn

_____   17. New and unusual thing

_____   18. Napping

_____   19. Hit with a sharp blow

_____   20. Imitation

Rumble Fish Vocabulary Fill In The Blanks 2 Answer Key

ALLIES	1. Supporters; partners
TINGE	2. Small amount of color
RASPING	3. Harsh, grating sound
EVENTUALLY	4. Finally
SASSY	5. Lively
ATHEIST	6. One who does not believe in God
SCOWLING	7. Looking angry by lowering the eyebrows
SCROUNGING	8. Searching
OBNOXIOUS	9. Offensive; annoying
STALKING	10. Walking in an angry manner
DAZEDLY	11. In a confused manner
ABANDONED	12. Deserted; left
PERCEPTION	13. Insight
CONTRARY	14. Opposite
CAUTIOUS	15. Careful
INNATE	16. Inherited; inborn
NOVELTY	17. New and unusual thing
DOZING	18. Napping
CLIPPED	19. Hit with a sharp blow
SIMULATED	20. Imitation

Rumble Fish Vocabulary Fill In The Blanks 3

_____ 1. Opposite

_____ 2. Looking angry by lowering the eyebrows

_____ 3. Uncivilized; simple

_____ 4. Hit with a sharp blow

_____ 5. Finally

_____ 6. Empty

_____ 7. Insight

_____ 8. Anxiety; unease

_____ 9. In a confused manner

_____ 10. One who does not believe in God

_____ 11. Harsh, grating sound

_____ 12. Lively

_____ 13. Mocking

_____ 14. Aching

_____ 15. Choice

_____ 16. Deserted; left

_____ 17. Deformed; twisted out of shape

_____ 18. Napping

_____ 19. Intense

_____ 20. Permit; endure

Rumble Fish Vocabulary Fill In The Blanks 3 Answer Key

CONTRARY	1. Opposite
SCOWLING	2. Looking angry by lowering the eyebrows
PRIMITIVE	3. Uncivilized; simple
CLIPPED	4. Hit with a sharp blow
EVENTUALLY	5. Finally
VACANT	6. Empty
PERCEPTION	7. Insight
TENSION	8. Anxiety; unease
DAZEDLY	9. In a confused manner
ATHEIST	10. One who does not believe in God
RASPING	11. Harsh, grating sound
SASSY	12. Lively
SARCASTIC	13. Mocking
THROBBING	14. Aching
ALTERNATIVE	15. Choice
ABANDONED	16. Deserted; left
DISTORTED	17. Deformed; twisted out of shape
DOZING	18. Napping
ACUTE	19. Intense
TOLERATE	20. Permit; endure

Rumble Fish Vocabulary Fill In The Blanks 4

_____ 1. Finally

_____ 2. Aching

_____ 3. Empty

_____ 4. Permit; endure

_____ 5. Napping

_____ 6. Person who worships many gods

_____ 7. Bothered; annoyed

_____ 8. Choice

_____ 9. A period of time

_____ 10. Lively

_____ 11. Madman; lunatic

_____ 12. Difficult; involved

_____ 13. Searching

_____ 14. Alone; single

_____ 15. Deformed; twisted out of shape

_____ 16. In a confused manner

_____ 17. Uncivilized; simple

_____ 18. Hit with a sharp blow

_____ 19. Imitation

_____ 20. New and unusual thing

Rumble Fish Vocabulary Fill In The Blanks 4 Answer Key

EVENTUALLY	1. Finally
THROBBING	2. Aching
VACANT	3. Empty
TOLERATE	4. Permit; endure
DOZING	5. Napping
PAGAN	6. Person who worships many gods
PESTERED	7. Bothered; annoyed
ALTERNATIVE	8. Choice
ERA	9. A period of time
SASSY	10. Lively
MANIAC	11. Madman; lunatic
COMPLICATED	12. Difficult; involved
SCROUNGING	13. Searching
SOLITARY	14. Alone; single
DISTORTED	15. Deformed; twisted out of shape
DAZEDLY	16. In a confused manner
PRIMITIVE	17. Uncivilized; simple
CLIPPED	18. Hit with a sharp blow
SIMULATED	19. Imitation
NOVELTY	20. New and unusual thing

Rumble Fish Vocabulary Matching 1

___ 1. TOLERATE   A. Permit; endure
___ 2. THROBBING   B. New and unusual thing
___ 3. STALKING   C. Madman; lunatic
___ 4. OBNOXIOUS   D. Careful
___ 5. ACUTE   E. Walking in an angry manner
___ 6. ALLIES   F. Deformed; twisted out of shape
___ 7. SIMULATED   G. Inherited; inborn
___ 8. COMPLICATED   H. Imitation
___ 9. SOLITARY   I. Difficult; involved
___10. NOVELTY   J. Harsh, grating sound
___11. RASPING   K. Hit with a sharp blow
___12. INNATE   L. Choice
___13. CLIPPED   M. Supporters; partners
___14. PAGAN   N. Offensive; annoying
___15. MISCAST   O. Looking angry by lowering the eyebrows
___16. CONTRARY   P. Person who worships many gods
___17. PRECEDENT   Q. Searching
___18. SCROUNGING   R. Alone; single
___19. CAUTIOUS   S. Example for future actions
___20. ERA   T. A period of time
___21. SCOWLING   U. Put in an unsuitable role
___22. MANIAC   V. Aching
___23. PERCEPTION   W. Insight
___24. ALTERNATIVE   X. Intense
___25. DISTORTED   Y. Opposite

Rumble Fish Vocabulary Matching 1 Answer Key

A - 1.	TOLERATE	A.	Permit; endure
V - 2.	THROBBING	B.	New and unusual thing
E - 3.	STALKING	C.	Madman; lunatic
N - 4.	OBNOXIOUS	D.	Careful
X - 5.	ACUTE	E.	Walking in an angry manner
M - 6.	ALLIES	F.	Deformed; twisted out of shape
H - 7.	SIMULATED	G.	Inherited; inborn
I - 8.	COMPLICATED	H.	Imitation
R - 9.	SOLITARY	I.	Difficult; involved
B - 10.	NOVELTY	J.	Harsh, grating sound
J - 11.	RASPING	K.	Hit with a sharp blow
G - 12.	INNATE	L.	Choice
K - 13.	CLIPPED	M.	Supporters; partners
P - 14.	PAGAN	N.	Offensive; annoying
U - 15.	MISCAST	O.	Looking angry by lowering the eyebrows
Y - 16.	CONTRARY	P.	Person who worships many gods
S - 17.	PRECEDENT	Q.	Searching
Q - 18.	SCROUNGING	R.	Alone; single
D - 19.	CAUTIOUS	S.	Example for future actions
T - 20.	ERA	T.	A period of time
O - 21.	SCOWLING	U.	Put in an unsuitable role
C - 22.	MANIAC	V.	Aching
W - 23.	PERCEPTION	W.	Insight
L - 24.	ALTERNATIVE	X.	Intense
F - 25.	DISTORTED	Y.	Opposite

Rumble Fish Vocabulary Matching 2

___ 1. ALTERNATIVE   A. Madman; lunatic
___ 2. PRECEDENT   B. Aching
___ 3. MANIAC   C. Supporters; partners
___ 4. DISTORTED   D. Finally
___ 5. PRIMITIVE   E. Careful
___ 6. EVENTUALLY   F. Permit; endure
___ 7. DOZING   G. Alone; single
___ 8. SCOWLING   H. Inherited; inborn
___ 9. THROBBING   I. Hit with a sharp blow
___10. SIMULATED   J. Offensive; annoying
___11. ABANDONED   K. Looking angry by lowering the eyebrows
___12. ATHEIST   L. Uncivilized; simple
___13. TOLERATE   M. Example for future actions
___14. INNATE   N. Empty
___15. SOLITARY   O. Deserted; left
___16. MISCAST   P. Insight
___17. CONTRARY   Q. Choice
___18. VACANT   R. One who does not believe in God
___19. OBNOXIOUS   S. Napping
___20. ALLIES   T. Imitation
___21. PESTERED   U. Deformed; twisted out of shape
___22. TENSION   V. Opposite
___23. PERCEPTION   W. Put in an unsuitable role
___24. CAUTIOUS   X. Anxiety; unease
___25. CLIPPED   Y. Bothered; annoyed

Rumble Fish Vocabulary Matching 2 Answer Key

Q - 1.	ALTERNATIVE	A.	Madman; lunatic
M - 2.	PRECEDENT	B.	Aching
A - 3.	MANIAC	C.	Supporters; partners
U - 4.	DISTORTED	D.	Finally
L - 5.	PRIMITIVE	E.	Careful
D - 6.	EVENTUALLY	F.	Permit; endure
S - 7.	DOZING	G.	Alone; single
K - 8.	SCOWLING	H.	Inherited; inborn
B - 9.	THROBBING	I.	Hit with a sharp blow
T - 10.	SIMULATED	J.	Offensive; annoying
O - 11.	ABANDONED	K.	Looking angry by lowering the eyebrows
R - 12.	ATHEIST	L.	Uncivilized; simple
F - 13.	TOLERATE	M.	Example for future actions
H - 14.	INNATE	N.	Empty
G - 15.	SOLITARY	O.	Deserted; left
W - 16.	MISCAST	P.	Insight
V - 17.	CONTRARY	Q.	Choice
N - 18.	VACANT	R.	One who does not believe in God
J - 19.	OBNOXIOUS	S.	Napping
C - 20.	ALLIES	T.	Imitation
Y - 21.	PESTERED	U.	Deformed; twisted out of shape
X - 22.	TENSION	V.	Opposite
P - 23.	PERCEPTION	W.	Put in an unsuitable role
E - 24.	CAUTIOUS	X.	Anxiety; unease
I - 25.	CLIPPED	Y.	Bothered; annoyed

Rumble Fish Vocabulary Matching 3

___ 1. VACANT   A. Opposite
___ 2. DAZEDLY   B. Choice
___ 3. TENSION   C. Insight
___ 4. ALTERNATIVE   D. Madman; lunatic
___ 5. MANIAC   E. In a confused manner
___ 6. DOZING   F. Searching
___ 7. PERCEPTION   G. Difficult; involved
___ 8. SUPERELITE   H. Supporters; partners
___ 9. ALLIES   I. Napping
___10. TINGE   J. Careful
___11. SCROUNGING   K. High-fashion
___12. SIMULATED   L. Looking angry by lowering the eyebrows
___13. COMPLICATED   M. Deserted; left
___14. PRIMITIVE   N. New and unusual thing
___15. TOLERATE   O. Imitation
___16. DISTORTED   P. One who does not believe in God
___17. NOVELTY   Q. Offensive; annoying
___18. MISCAST   R. Empty
___19. CAUTIOUS   S. Small amount of color
___20. OBNOXIOUS   T. Anxiety; unease
___21. ACUTE   U. Put in an unsuitable role
___22. ATHEIST   V. Permit; endure
___23. CONTRARY   W. Deformed; twisted out of shape
___24. SCOWLING   X. Uncivilized; simple
___25. ABANDONED   Y. Intense

Rumble Fish Vocabulary Matching 3 Answer Key

R - 1. VACANT
E - 2. DAZEDLY
T - 3. TENSION
B - 4. ALTERNATIVE
D - 5. MANIAC
I - 6. DOZING
C - 7. PERCEPTION
K - 8. SUPERELITE
H - 9. ALLIES
S - 10. TINGE
F - 11. SCROUNGING
O - 12. SIMULATED
G - 13. COMPLICATED
X - 14. PRIMITIVE
V - 15. TOLERATE
W - 16. DISTORTED
N - 17. NOVELTY
U - 18. MISCAST
J - 19. CAUTIOUS
Q - 20. OBNOXIOUS
Y - 21. ACUTE
P - 22. ATHEIST
A - 23. CONTRARY
L - 24. SCOWLING
M - 25. ABANDONED

A. Opposite
B. Choice
C. Insight
D. Madman; lunatic
E. In a confused manner
F. Searching
G. Difficult; involved
H. Supporters; partners
I. Napping
J. Careful
K. High-fashion
L. Looking angry by lowering the eyebrows
M. Deserted; left
N. New and unusual thing
O. Imitation
P. One who does not believe in God
Q. Offensive; annoying
R. Empty
S. Small amount of color
T. Anxiety; unease
U. Put in an unsuitable role
V. Permit; endure
W. Deformed; twisted out of shape
X. Uncivilized; simple
Y. Intense

Rumble Fish Vocabulary Matching 4

___ 1. COMPLICATED   A. Choice
___ 2. CLIPPED   B. Napping
___ 3. PERCEPTION   C. Madman; lunatic
___ 4. ALLIES   D. A period of time
___ 5. ERA   E. Supporters; partners
___ 6. SASSY   F. Lively
___ 7. INNATE   G. Harsh, grating sound
___ 8. DOZING   H. Hit with a sharp blow
___ 9. ABANDONED   I. Permit; endure
___10. NOVELTY   J. Deserted; left
___11. MISCAST   K. Anxiety; unease
___12. SUPERELITE   L. Finally
___13. DAZEDLY   M. Empty
___14. TOLERATE   N. Put in an unsuitable role
___15. CAUTIOUS   O. Inherited; inborn
___16. TENSION   P. Careful
___17. MANIAC   Q. High-fashion
___18. SOLITARY   R. In a confused manner
___19. TINGE   S. Insight
___20. RASPING   T. Difficult; involved
___21. STALKING   U. Walking in an angry manner
___22. VACANT   V. New and unusual thing
___23. ALTERNATIVE   W. Mocking
___24. EVENTUALLY   X. Small amount of color
___25. SARCASTIC   Y. Alone; single

Rumble Fish Vocabulary Matching 4 Answer Key

T - 1. COMPLICATED	A. Choice
H - 2. CLIPPED	B. Napping
S - 3. PERCEPTION	C. Madman; lunatic
E - 4. ALLIES	D. A period of time
D - 5. ERA	E. Supporters; partners
F - 6. SASSY	F. Lively
O - 7. INNATE	G. Harsh, grating sound
B - 8. DOZING	H. Hit with a sharp blow
J - 9. ABANDONED	I. Permit; endure
V - 10. NOVELTY	J. Deserted; left
N - 11. MISCAST	K. Anxiety; unease
Q - 12. SUPERELITE	L. Finally
R - 13. DAZEDLY	M. Empty
I - 14. TOLERATE	N. Put in an unsuitable role
P - 15. CAUTIOUS	O. Inherited; inborn
K - 16. TENSION	P. Careful
C - 17. MANIAC	Q. High-fashion
Y - 18. SOLITARY	R. In a confused manner
X - 19. TINGE	S. Insight
G - 20. RASPING	T. Difficult; involved
U - 21. STALKING	U. Walking in an angry manner
M - 22. VACANT	V. New and unusual thing
A - 23. ALTERNATIVE	W. Mocking
L - 24. EVENTUALLY	X. Small amount of color
W - 25. SARCASTIC	Y. Alone; single

Rumble Fish Vocabulary Magic Squares 1

Match the definition with the vocabulary word. Put your answers in the magic squares below. When your answers are correct, all columns and rows will add to the same number.

A. MISCAST
B. ALTERNATIVE
C. INNATE
D. TENSION
E. MANIAC
F. SOLITARY
G. CAUTIOUS
H. THROBBING
I. PERCEPTION
J. PRIMITIVE
K. VACANT
L. SIMULATED
M. CLIPPED
N. EVENTUALLY
O. COMPLICATED
P. ERA

1. Alone; single
2. Insight
3. Difficult; involved
4. Anxiety; unease
5. Hit with a sharp blow
6. Choice
7. Aching
8. Empty
9. Inherited; inborn
10. A period of time
11. Uncivilized; simple
12. Madman; lunatic
13. Imitation
14. Careful
15. Put in an unsuitable role
16. Finally

A=	B=	C=	D=
E=	F=	G=	H=
I=	J=	K=	L=
M=	N=	O=	P=

Rumble Fish Vocabulary Magic Squares 1 Answer Key

Match the definition with the vocabulary word. Put your answers in the magic squares below. When your answers are correct, all columns and rows will add to the same number.

A. MISCAST
B. ALTERNATIVE
C. INNATE
D. TENSION
E. MANIAC
F. SOLITARY
G. CAUTIOUS
H. THROBBING
I. PERCEPTION
J. PRIMITIVE
K. VACANT
L. SIMULATED
M. CLIPPED
N. EVENTUALLY
O. COMPLICATED
P. ERA

1. Alone; single
2. Insight
3. Difficult; involved
4. Anxiety; unease
5. Hit with a sharp blow
6. Choice
7. Aching
8. Empty
9. Inherited; inborn
10. A period of time
11. Uncivilized; simple
12. Madman; lunatic
13. Imitation
14. Careful
15. Put in an unsuitable role
16. Finally

A=15	B=6	C=9	D=4
E=12	F=1	G=14	H=7
I=2	J=11	K=8	L=13
M=5	N=16	O=3	P=10

Rumble Fish Vocabulary Magic Squares 2

Match the definition with the vocabulary word. Put your answers in the magic squares below. When your answers are correct, all columns and rows will add to the same number.

A. SIMULATED   E. SARCASTIC   I. TINGE   M. PESTERED
B. SCOWLING   F. PERCEPTION   J. DISTORTED   N. RASPING
C. PRECEDENT   G. EVENTUALLY   K. SCROUNGING   O. ACUTE
D. SOLITARY   H. THROBBING   L. PRIMITIVE   P. CLIPPED

1. Bothered; annoyed
2. Insight
3. Aching
4. Intense
5. Uncivilized; simple
6. Example for future actions
7. Imitation
8. Deformed; twisted out of shape
9. Searching
10. Alone; single
11. Looking angry by lowering the eyebrows
12. Small amount of color
13. Harsh, grating sound
14. Mocking
15. Finally
16. Hit with a sharp blow

A=	B=	C=	D=
E=	F=	G=	H=
I=	J=	K=	L=
M=	N=	O=	P=

Rumble Fish Vocabulary Magic Squares 2 Answer Key

Match the definition with the vocabulary word. Put your answers in the magic squares below. When your answers are correct, all columns and rows will add to the same number.

A. SIMULATED
B. SCOWLING
C. PRECEDENT
D. SOLITARY
E. SARCASTIC
F. PERCEPTION
G. EVENTUALLY
H. THROBBING
I. TINGE
J. DISTORTED
K. SCROUNGING
L. PRIMITIVE
M. PESTERED
N. RASPING
O. ACUTE
P. CLIPPED

1. Bothered; annoyed
2. Insight
3. Aching
4. Intense
5. Uncivilized; simple
6. Example for future actions
7. Imitation
8. Deformed; twisted out of shape
9. Searching
10. Alone; single
11. Looking angry by lowering the eyebrows
12. Small amount of color
13. Harsh, grating sound
14. Mocking
15. Finally
16. Hit with a sharp blow

A=7	B=11	C=6	D=10
E=14	F=2	G=15	H=3
I=12	J=8	K=9	L=5
M=1	N=13	O=4	P=16

Rumble Fish Vocabulary Magic Squares 3

Match the definition with the vocabulary word. Put your answers in the magic squares below. When your answers are correct, all columns and rows will add to the same number.

A. INNATE
B. CLIPPED
C. VACANT
D. OBNOXIOUS
E. COMPLICATED
F. EVENTUALLY
G. THROBBING
H. PRIMITIVE
I. MISCAST
J. CONTRARY
K. SASSY
L. MANIAC
M. ERA
N. TOLERATE
O. ALLIES
P. STALKING

1. Uncivilized; simple
2. A period of time
3. Hit with a sharp blow
4. Lively
5. Opposite
6. Empty
7. Walking in an angry manner
8. Difficult; involved
9. Supporters; partners
10. Finally
11. Put in an unsuitable role
12. Offensive; annoying
13. Inherited; inborn
14. Madman; lunatic
15. Aching
16. Permit; endure

A=	B=	C=	D=
E=	F=	G=	H=
I=	J=	K=	L=
M=	N=	O=	P=

Rumble Fish Vocabulary Magic Squares 3 Answer Key

Match the definition with the vocabulary word. Put your answers in the magic squares below. When your answers are correct, all columns and rows will add to the same number.

A. INNATE
B. CLIPPED
C. VACANT
D. OBNOXIOUS
E. COMPLICATED
F. EVENTUALLY
G. THROBBING
H. PRIMITIVE
I. MISCAST
J. CONTRARY
K. SASSY
L. MANIAC
M. ERA
N. TOLERATE
O. ALLIES
P. STALKING

1. Uncivilized; simple
2. A period of time
3. Hit with a sharp blow
4. Lively
5. Opposite
6. Empty
7. Walking in an angry manner
8. Difficult; involved
9. Supporters; partners
10. Finally
11. Put in an unsuitable role
12. Offensive; annoying
13. Inherited; inborn
14. Madman; lunatic
15. Aching
16. Permit; endure

A=13	B=3	C=6	D=12
E=8	F=10	G=15	H=1
I=11	J=5	K=4	L=14
M=2	N=16	O=9	P=7

Rumble Fish Vocabulary Magic Squares 4

Match the definition with the vocabulary word. Put your answers in the magic squares below. When your answers are correct, all columns and rows will add to the same number.

A. SUPERELITE   E. DISTORTED   I. PESTERED   M. NOVELTY
B. INNATE   F. CLIPPED   J. DOZING   N. SOLITARY
C. SIMULATED   G. ATHEIST   K. PERCEPTION   O. SCROUNGING
D. CONTRARY   H. COMPLICATED   L. DAZEDLY   P. THROBBING

1. Searching
2. Napping
3. Difficult; involved
4. High-fashion
5. Opposite
6. Deformed; twisted out of shape
7. Insight
8. Alone; single
9. Hit with a sharp blow
10. Imitation
11. New and unusual thing
12. In a confused manner
13. Bothered; annoyed
14. Aching
15. Inherited; inborn
16. One who does not believe in God

A=	B=	C=	D=
E=	F=	G=	H=
I=	J=	K=	L=
M=	N=	O=	P=

Rumble Fish Vocabulary Magic Squares 4 Answer Key

Match the definition with the vocabulary word. Put your answers in the magic squares below. When your answers are correct, all columns and rows will add to the same number.

A. SUPERELITE
B. INNATE
C. SIMULATED
D. CONTRARY
E. DISTORTED
F. CLIPPED
G. ATHEIST
H. COMPLICATED
I. PESTERED
J. DOZING
K. PERCEPTION
L. DAZEDLY
M. NOVELTY
N. SOLITARY
O. SCROUNGING
P. THROBBING

1. Searching
2. Napping
3. Difficult; involved
4. High-fashion
5. Opposite
6. Deformed; twisted out of shape
7. Insight
8. Alone; single
9. Hit with a sharp blow
10. Imitation
11. New and unusual thing
12. In a confused manner
13. Bothered; annoyed
14. Aching
15. Inherited; inborn
16. One who does not believe in God

A=4	B=15	C=10	D=5
E=6	F=9	G=16	H=3
I=13	J=2	K=7	L=12
M=11	N=8	O=1	P=14

Rumble Fish Vocabulary Word Search 1

Words are placed backwards, forward, diagonally, up and down. Clues listed below can help you find the words. Circle the hidden vocabulary words in the maze.

```
S X C D A Z E D L Y Y R A R T N O C P G
W I O E S B N R H S A C L D O O T I R L
R Y M S V O A M N S P A L I L V H T E J
A D P U G E L N P A K I I S E E R S C D
L F L O L C N I D S D N E T R L O A E S
T S I I K A N T T O N A S O A T B C D G
E Q C X W G T Q U A N M M R T Y B R E F
R C A O R C E E T A R E B T E G I A N C
N N T N W P N E D F L Y D E T N N S T B
A W E B D L S F H H W L V D I I G S B V
T S D O V K I M Z L F S Y X L K X T C B
I C C K K V O N W P U T L X E L B N F H
V H J K Z D N T G O H L L K R A C B T M
E S C R O U N G I N G D E R E T S E P M
G J K R C Y J T R Z J N B J P S N T C M
M P R P Z T U D D L O N K G U N S J V R
N L M P P A Z L L I D C K D S A L Q Q Z
L F C T C E V N T T D D P G C C Q C Q N
D Z Y N Z T N P S Q E W H S Y M G Z E F
O N X V T U E G J P V Z I Y T Y L B R N
Z N T N A C A V P R I M I T I V E D A G
I G Q V R A Y I X F S Q F V N L C G N F
N H Q E R Z L W P S H T G Z G Q A P F B
G D P D Z C A T H E I S T D E P R Y Y F
```

A period of time (3)
Aching (9)
Alone; single (8)
Anxiety; unease (7)
Bothered; annoyed (8)
Careful (8)
Choice (11)
Deformed; twisted out of shape (9)
Deserted; left (9)
Difficult; involved (11)
Empty (6)
Example for future actions (9)
Finally (10)
Harsh, grating sound (7)
High-fashion (10)
Hit with a sharp blow (7)
Imitation (9)
In a confused manner (7)
Inherited; inborn (6)
Insight (10)

Intense (5)
Lively (5)
Looking angry by lowering the eyebrows (8)
Madman; lunatic (6)
Mocking (9)
Napping (6)
New and unusual thing (7)
Offensive; annoying (9)
One who does not believe in God (7)
Opposite (8)
Permit; endure (8)
Person who worships many gods (5)
Put in an unsuitable role (7)
Searching (10)
Small amount of color (5)
Supporters; partners (6)
Uncivilized; simple (9)
Walking in an angry manner (8)

Rumble Fish Vocabulary Word Search 1 Answer Key

Words are placed backwards, forward, diagonally, up and down. Clues listed below can help you find the words. Circle the hidden vocabulary words in the maze.

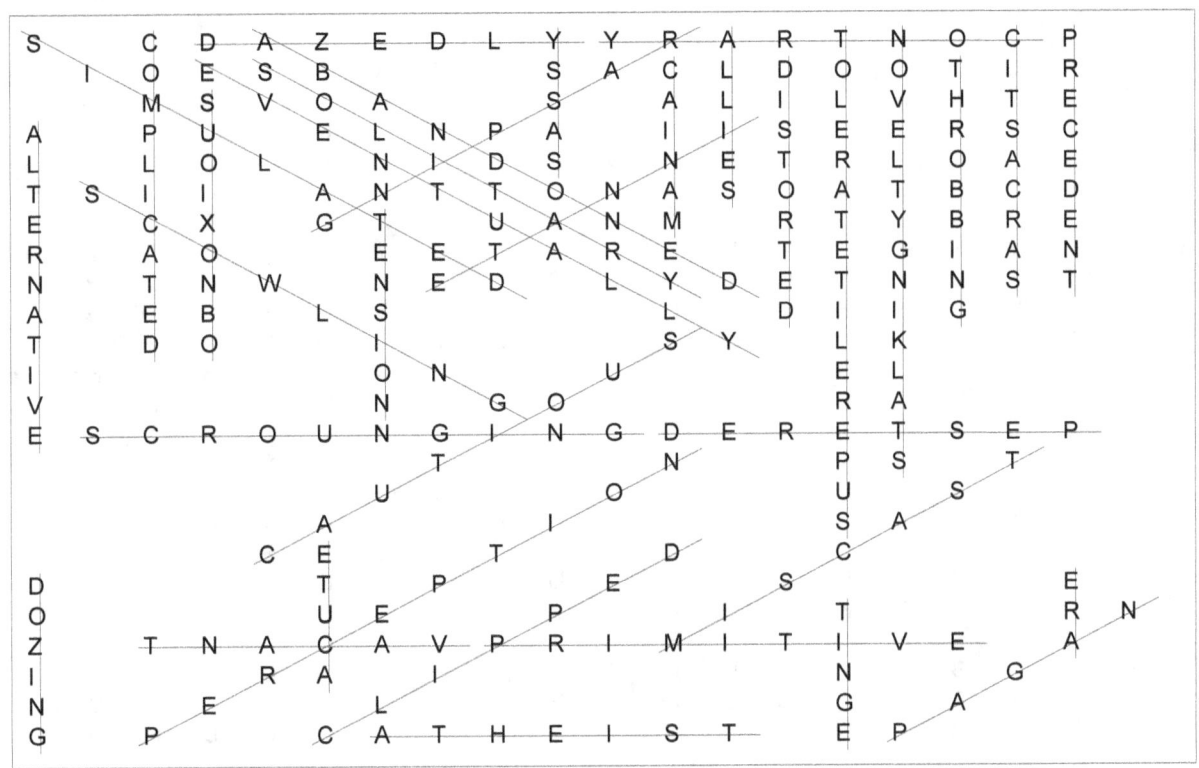

A period of time (3)
Aching (9)
Alone; single (8)
Anxiety; unease (7)
Bothered; annoyed (8)
Careful (8)
Choice (11)
Deformed; twisted out of shape (9)
Deserted; left (9)
Difficult; involved (11)
Empty (6)
Example for future actions (9)
Finally (10)
Harsh, grating sound (7)
High-fashion (10)
Hit with a sharp blow (7)
Imitation (9)
In a confused manner (7)
Inherited; inborn (6)
Insight (10)

Intense (5)
Lively (5)
Looking angry by lowering the eyebrows (8)
Madman; lunatic (6)
Mocking (9)
Napping (6)
New and unusual thing (7)
Offensive; annoying (9)
One who does not believe in God (7)
Opposite (8)
Permit; endure (8)
Person who worships many gods (5)
Put in an unsuitable role (7)
Searching (10)
Small amount of color (5)
Supporters; partners (6)
Uncivilized; simple (9)
Walking in an angry manner (8)

Rumble Fish Vocabulary Word Search 2

Words are placed backwards, forward, diagonally, up and down. Clues listed below can help you find the words. Circle the hidden vocabulary words in the maze.

```
C P P A G A N S U P E R E L I T E A S W
C O R G B F F S O F X Z C T R O V C I P
Z D M I K A F M P L C Q Z B B L E U M M
V M I P M T N M B P I G Z T D E N T U B
H A S V L I F D R L M T S P B R T E L C
W N C Q N I T E O N W I A E P A U C A R
D I A A N K C I F N E B D R X T A O T S
S A S V N E D A V H E D N C Y E L N E T
C C T X D T O N T E L D P E L Z L T D R
O S G E C P Z A Y E Q L Y P T Q Y R M G
W S N B S O I L N Z D M Z T V G C A W Q
L T S K A B N T H R O B B I N G L R M F
I A C P S N G E L B X C W O M P D Y B B
N L R Q S O D R G K P A S N K P Y S N K
G K O X Y X M N A Y D U F L P K S H O J
F I U V L I N A L S M T D B Q A K V V P
R N N K Y O L T L B P I K A R M J P E T
L G G P I U N I I X J O G C Z N S C L Z
N N I S C S H V E H V U A V P E M Q T T
I N N A T E K E S P E S T E R E D P Y L
L E G F G Y Y Y B R T J N A V J K L Y Q
T D J N B M Y T D I S T O R T E D K Y P
Z B I K B L G G C M N R A S P I N G C B
X T W Q B W N P C N J C L I P P E D M R
```

A period of time (3)
Aching (9)
Alone; single (8)
Anxiety; unease (7)
Bothered; annoyed (8)
Careful (8)
Choice (11)
Deformed; twisted out of shape (9)
Deserted; left (9)
Difficult; involved (11)
Empty (6)
Example for future actions (9)
Finally (10)
Harsh, grating sound (7)
High-fashion (10)
Hit with a sharp blow (7)
Imitation (9)
In a confused manner (7)
Inherited; inborn (6)
Insight (10)

Intense (5)
Lively (5)
Looking angry by lowering the eyebrows (8)
Madman; lunatic (6)
Mocking (9)
Napping (6)
New and unusual thing (7)
Offensive; annoying (9)
One who does not believe in God (7)
Opposite (8)
Permit; endure (8)
Person who worships many gods (5)
Put in an unsuitable role (7)
Searching (10)
Small amount of color (5)
Supporters; partners (6)
Uncivilized; simple (9)
Walking in an angry manner (8)

Rumble Fish Vocabulary Word Search 2 Answer Key

Words are placed backwards, forward, diagonally, up and down. Clues listed below can help you find the words. Circle the hidden vocabulary words in the maze.

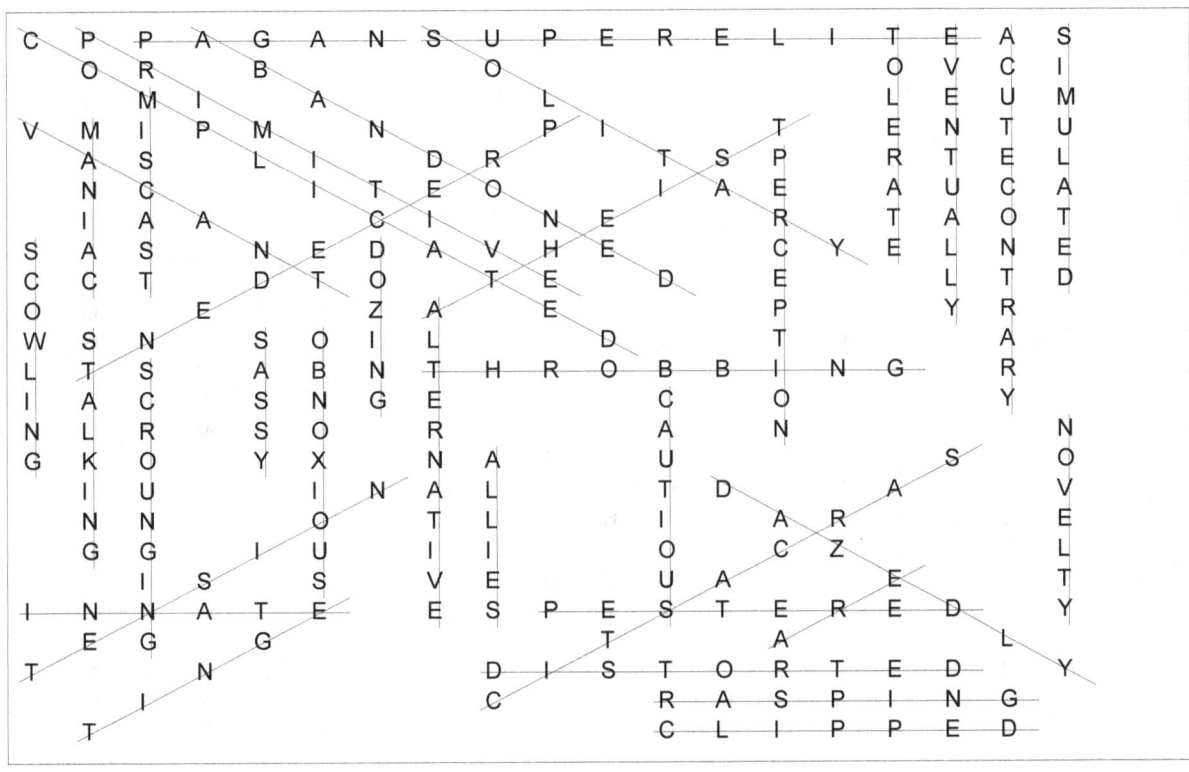

A period of time (3)
Aching (9)
Alone; single (8)
Anxiety; unease (7)
Bothered; annoyed (8)
Careful (8)
Choice (11)
Deformed; twisted out of shape (9)
Deserted; left (9)
Difficult; involved (11)
Empty (6)
Example for future actions (9)
Finally (10)
Harsh, grating sound (7)
High-fashion (10)
Hit with a sharp blow (7)
Imitation (9)
In a confused manner (7)
Inherited; inborn (6)
Insight (10)

Intense (5)
Lively (5)
Looking angry by lowering the eyebrows (8)
Madman; lunatic (6)
Mocking (9)
Napping (6)
New and unusual thing (7)
Offensive; annoying (9)
One who does not believe in God (7)
Opposite (8)
Permit; endure (8)
Person who worships many gods (5)
Put in an unsuitable role (7)
Searching (10)
Small amount of color (5)
Supporters; partners (6)
Uncivilized; simple (9)
Walking in an angry manner (8)

Rumble Fish Vocabulary Word Search 3

Words are placed backwards, forward, diagonally, up and down. Words listed below are included in the maze. Circle the hidden vocabulary words in the maze.

```
D C L I P P E D A Z E D L Y T A P A S L
S I C D K A H G K V E K L V H T R B O Y
A S S E H M G V V R B L V A R H I A L D
R C C T T Y Z A E H A P T C O E M N I F
C R O A O M P T N U K E B A B I I D T M
A O W C Y R S F T Y N R B N B S T O A F
S U L I P E T N Q S X C T T I T I N R S
T N I L P W E E I S C E N R N Y V E Y Y
I G N P D V N O D A J P E O G V E D L L
C I G M E V N S I S T T D P V X S Z X C
S N O O S K C N R B L I E Q C E H W C R
C G B C H T A C U T E O C Q O X L G N L
Q Z N W M M A L B T T N E F N D P T H T
Q H O H X M Q L T V B B R H T S Q M Y N
C Q X T D C R P K E R Q P Q R M X M P Y
P X I D P Z M W S I R C N M A L M F G C
Q N O X D K R C T I N N R V R G H D M Q
G S U D B V Q A L O M G A J Y G K G I F
S Z S O T H E U Z Y L U R T H S Y N S H
T J Y Z S T F T F R Y E L S I J L I C Z
W I T I A G K I K Q V M R A T V K P A T
F G N N J Z T O F Z Z G G A T G E S S X
B W N G X Q S U P E R E L I T E R A T C
C I Q N E Z Q S E I L L A T R E D R H B
```

ABANDONED	DISTORTED	PERCEPTION	SOLITARY
ACUTE	DOZING	PESTERED	STALKING
ALLIES	ERA	PRECEDENT	SUPERELITE
ALTERNATIVE	EVENTUALLY	PRIMITIVE	TENSION
ATHEIST	INNATE	RASPING	THROBBING
CAUTIOUS	MANIAC	SARCASTIC	TINGE
CLIPPED	MISCAST	SASSY	TOLERATE
COMPLICATED	NOVELTY	SCOWLING	VACANT
CONTRARY	OBNOXIOUS	SCROUNGING	
DAZEDLY	PAGAN	SIMULATED	

Rumble Fish Vocabulary Word Search 3 Answer Key

Words are placed backwards, forward, diagonally, up and down. Words listed below are included in the maze. Circle the hidden vocabulary words in the maze.

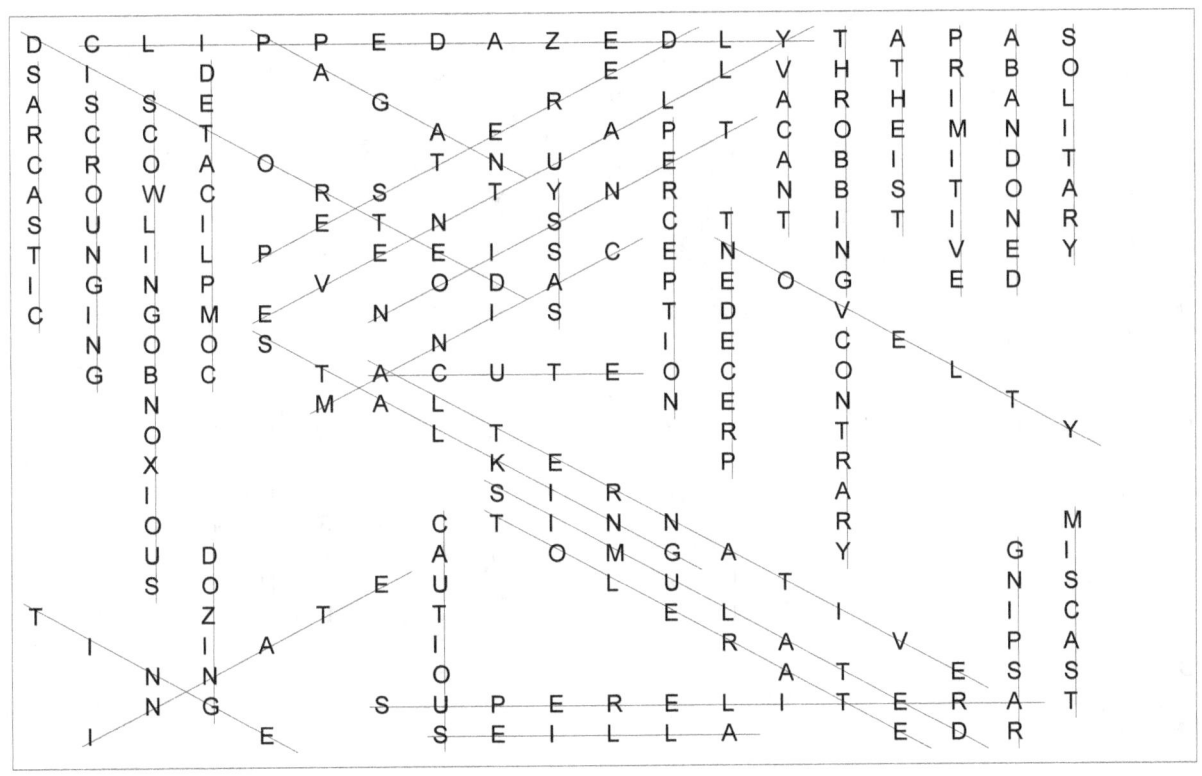

ABANDONED	DISTORTED	PERCEPTION	SOLITARY
ACUTE	DOZING	PESTERED	STALKING
ALLIES	ERA	PRECEDENT	SUPERELITE
ALTERNATIVE	EVENTUALLY	PRIMITIVE	TENSION
ATHEIST	INNATE	RASPING	THROBBING
CAUTIOUS	MANIAC	SARCASTIC	TINGE
CLIPPED	MISCAST	SASSY	TOLERATE
COMPLICATED	NOVELTY	SCOWLING	VACANT
CONTRARY	OBNOXIOUS	SCROUNGING	
DAZEDLY	PAGAN	SIMULATED	

Rumble Fish Vocabulary Word Search 4

Words are placed backwards, forward, diagonally, up and down. Words listed below are included in the maze. Circle the hidden vocabulary words in the maze.

```
S C R O U N G I N G B Y S S A S J Z E N
A G H Z K W L Z Q V L L Y S T N R V H M
R W W C R L W Y C L W L N V H G I A Z L
C L I P P E D R A S P I N G E T T B F W
A P W N R Z R U L J X X B H I H O A Z N
S E W L E T P N Z W S Q M S X L N Q C
T R Q X C N T Q Z H J D I X T D E D W B
I C S H E E V I T A N R E T L A R O C M
C E C V D N T C S H P M J B C G A N D R
M P E O E D H T O M T Y H B M Y T E E R
D T W D N Q L B L M D V M K R L E D T X
D I S V T T N S I N M I Y G S T Q A R
V O M G M O R G T P B Z S D S T I P L S
F N Q P X J N A A K D D C T A Q N T U S
T N X I H I C B R S N P A D O Z G P M Q
H H O P K H B A Y Y P E S T E R E D I Q
V U R L T K Z T U Q N C T D K R T D S L
S A A O L N L M R T O D B A E V A E L C
K T C J B E R A M W I H O L L N N J D Y
S B C A V B X Q L A S O I Z A L N X G L
K T L O N T I I L V N T U G I P I P T R
D P N J N T N N Z S E I A S F N C E Q Y
A C U T E G Q Y G J T P A Y K Y G J S H
C O M P L I C A T E D D G C S N Z F G Q
```

ABANDONED	DISTORTED	PERCEPTION	SOLITARY
ACUTE	DOZING	PESTERED	STALKING
ALLIES	ERA	PRECEDENT	SUPERELITE
ALTERNATIVE	EVENTUALLY	PRIMITIVE	TENSION
ATHEIST	INNATE	RASPING	THROBBING
CAUTIOUS	MANIAC	SARCASTIC	TINGE
CLIPPED	MISCAST	SASSY	TOLERATE
COMPLICATED	NOVELTY	SCOWLING	VACANT
CONTRARY	OBNOXIOUS	SCROUNGING	
DAZEDLY	PAGAN	SIMULATED	

Rumble Fish Vocabulary Word Search 4 Answer Key

Words are placed backwards, forward, diagonally, up and down. Words listed below are included in the maze. Circle the hidden vocabulary words in the maze.

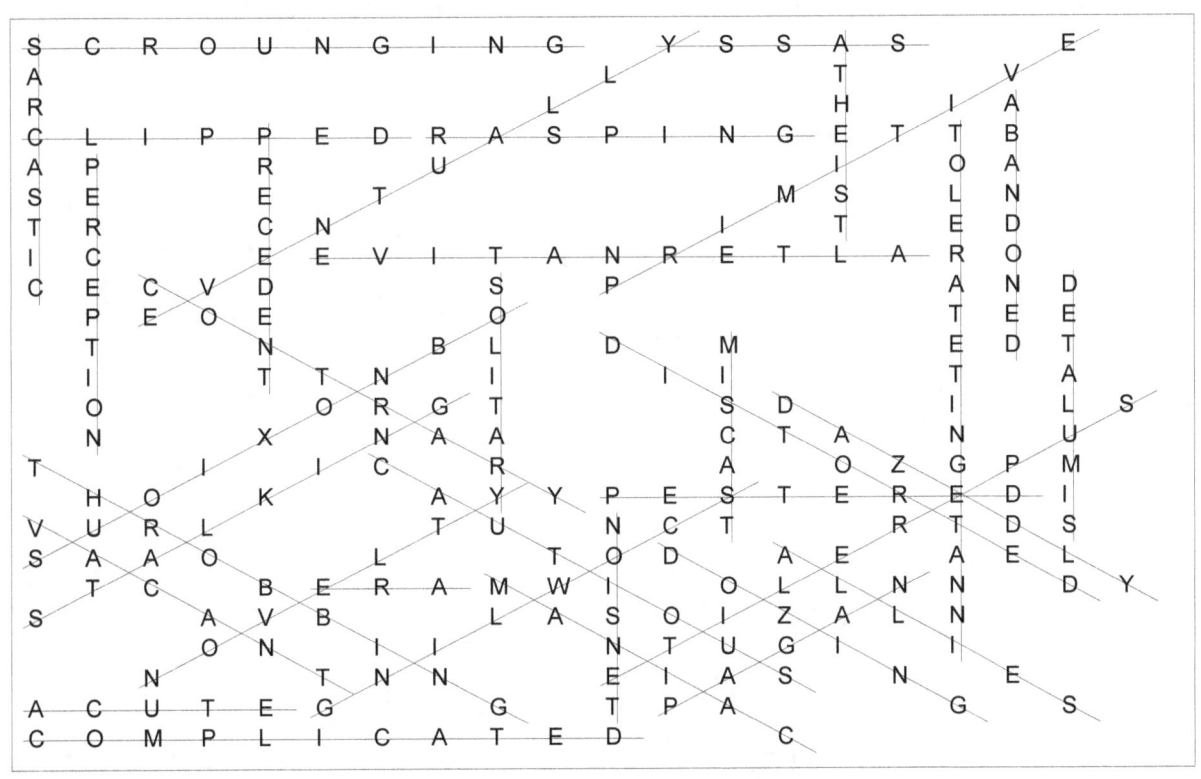

ABANDONED	DISTORTED	PERCEPTION	SOLITARY
ACUTE	DOZING	PESTERED	STALKING
ALLIES	ERA	PRECEDENT	SUPERELITE
ALTERNATIVE	EVENTUALLY	PRIMITIVE	TENSION
ATHEIST	INNATE	RASPING	THROBBING
CAUTIOUS	MANIAC	SARCASTIC	TINGE
CLIPPED	MISCAST	SASSY	TOLERATE
COMPLICATED	NOVELTY	SCOWLING	VACANT
CONTRARY	OBNOXIOUS	SCROUNGING	
DAZEDLY	PAGAN	SIMULATED	

Rumble Fish Vocabulary Crossword 1

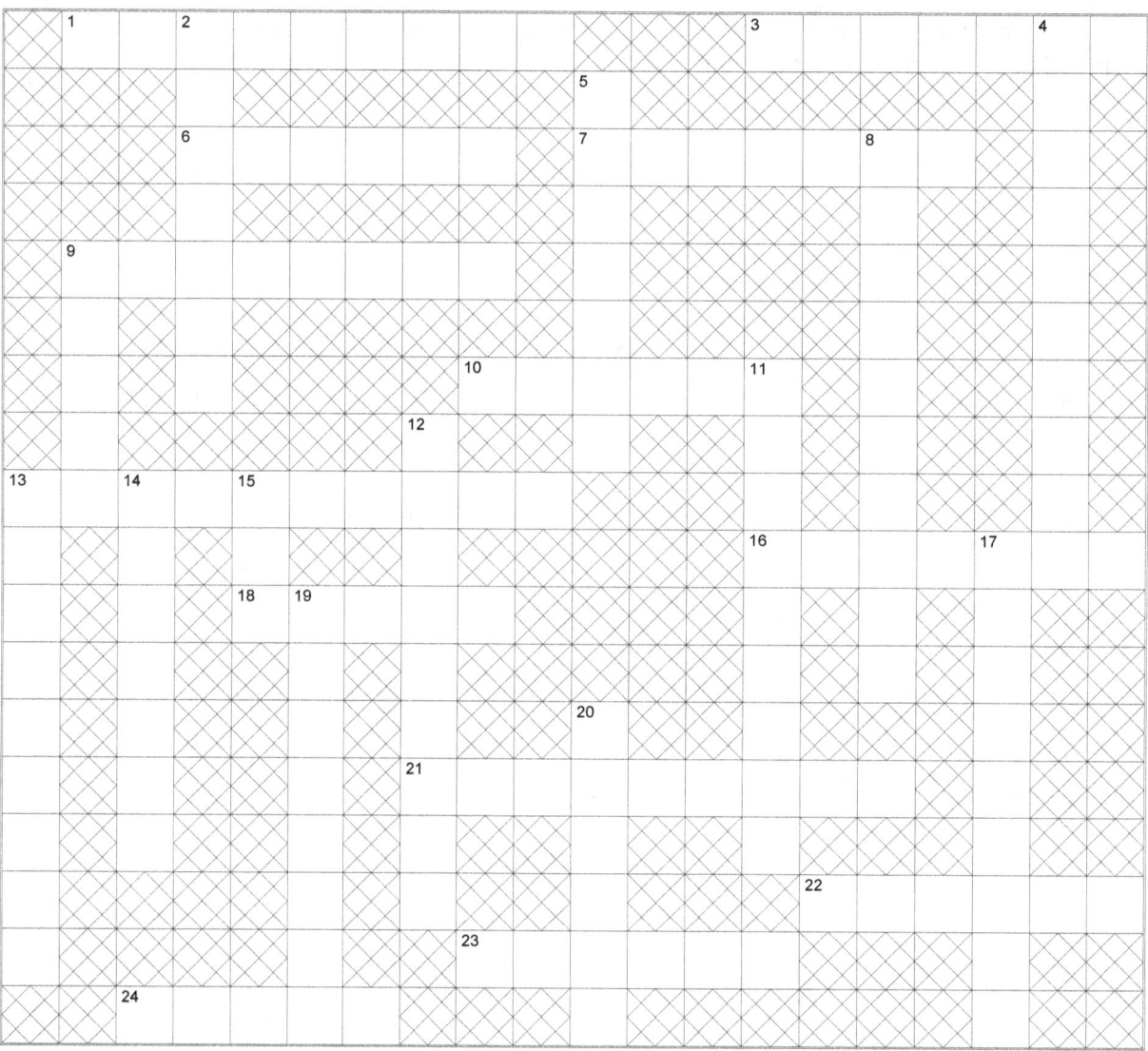

Across
1. Offensive; annoying
3. Put in an unsuitable role
6. Empty
7. One who does not believe in God
9. Permit; endure
10. Supporters; partners
13. Insight
16. Hit with a sharp blow
18. Intense
21. Aching
22. Madman; lunatic
23. Inherited; inborn
24. Lively

Down
2. New and unusual thing
4. High-fashion
5. In a confused manner
8. Searching
9. Small amount of color
11. Mocking
12. Deformed; twisted out of shape
13. Example for future actions
14. Harsh, grating sound
15. A period of time
17. Uncivilized; simple
19. Careful
20. Napping

Rumble Fish Vocabulary Crossword 1 Answer Key

Across
1. Offensive; annoying
3. Put in an unsuitable role
6. Empty
7. One who does not believe in God
9. Permit; endure
10. Supporters; partners
13. Insight
16. Hit with a sharp blow
18. Intense
21. Aching
22. Madman; lunatic
23. Inherited; inborn
24. Lively

Down
2. New and unusual thing
4. High-fashion
5. In a confused manner
8. Searching
9. Small amount of color
11. Mocking
12. Deformed; twisted out of shape
13. Example for future actions
14. Harsh, grating sound
15. A period of time
17. Uncivilized; simple
19. Careful
20. Napping

Rumble Fish Vocabulary Crossword 2

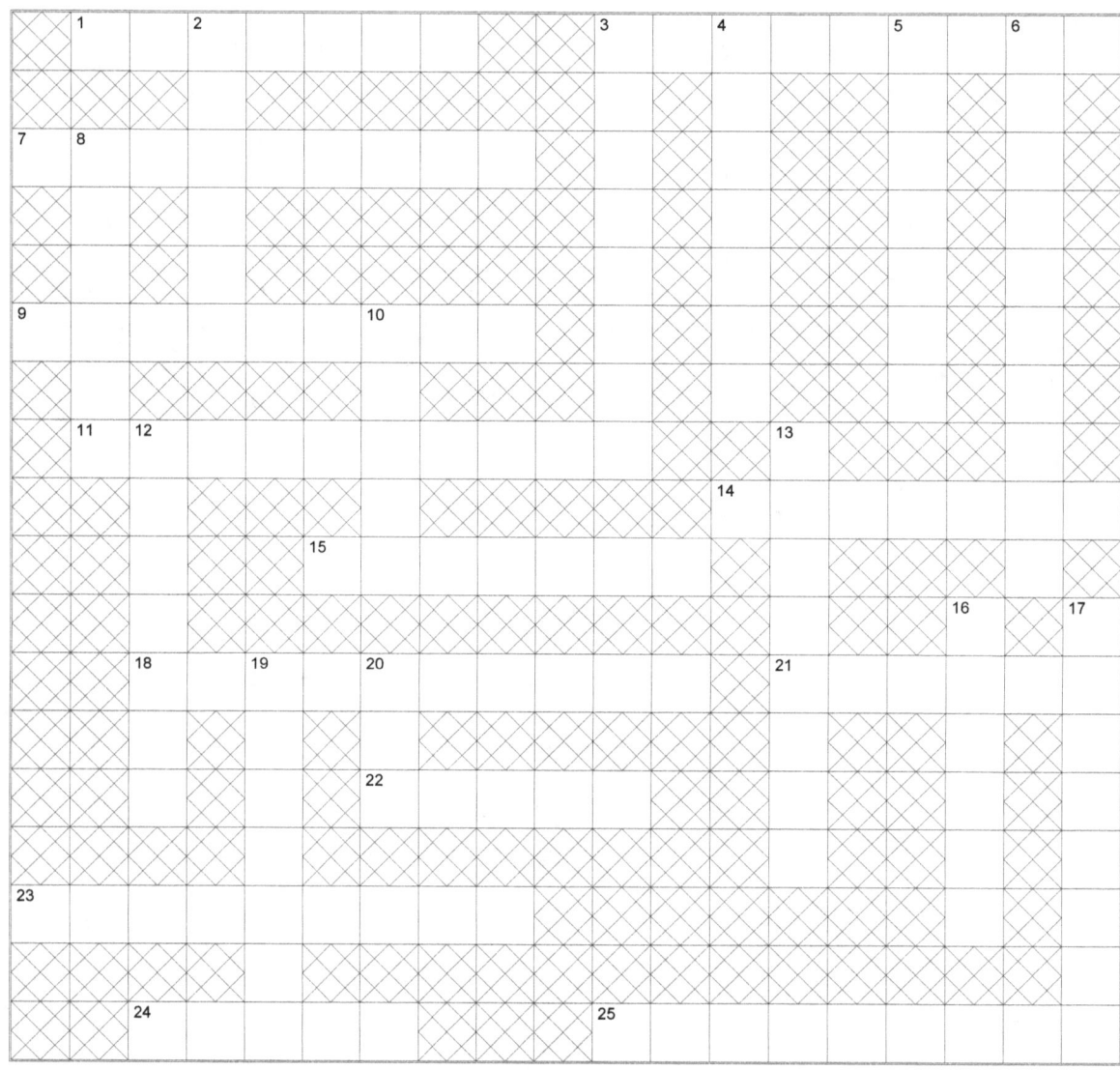

Across
1. New and unusual thing
3. Imitation
7. Mocking
9. Deformed; twisted out of shape
11. Searching
14. In a confused manner
15. Anxiety; unease
18. Insight
21. Inherited; inborn
22. Intense
23. Uncivilized; simple
24. Person who worships many gods
25. Deserted; left

Down
2. Empty
3. Looking angry by lowering the eyebrows
4. Put in an unsuitable role
5. One who does not believe in God
6. Finally
8. Supporters; partners
10. Small amount of color
12. Hit with a sharp blow
13. Careful
16. Madman; lunatic
17. Bothered; annoyed
19. Harsh, grating sound
20. A period of time

Rumble Fish Vocabulary Crossword 2 Answer Key

	1 N	2 V	E	L	T	Y		3 S	4 I	M	5 U	L	6 A	T	E	D
		A						C	I				T		V	
7 S	8 A	R	C	A	S	T	I	C		I	S		H		E	
	L							W			C		E		N	
	L		A					L			A		I		T	
9 D	I	S	T	O	10 R	T	E	D			S		S		U	
	E				I			N			T		T		A	
	11 S	12 C	R	O	U	N	G	I	N	G		13 C			L	
		L			G				14 D	A	Z	E	D	L	Y	
		I		15 T	E	N	S	I	O	N		U			Y	
		P							U			T		16 M		17 P
		18 P	19 E	R	20 C	E	P	T	I	O	N		21 I	N	N	A	T	E
			E		A				O				O		N		S
			D		22 A	C	U	T	E				U		I		T
					P								S		A		E
23 P	R	I	M	I	T	I	V	E							C		R
					N												E
		24 P	A	G	A	N			25 A	B	A	N	D	O	N	E	D

Across
1. New and unusual thing
3. Imitation
7. Mocking
9. Deformed; twisted out of shape
11. Searching
14. In a confused manner
15. Anxiety; unease
18. Insight
21. Inherited; inborn
22. Intense
23. Uncivilized; simple
24. Person who worships many gods
25. Deserted; left

Down
2. Empty
3. Looking angry by lowering the eyebrows
4. Put in an unsuitable role
5. One who does not believe in God
6. Finally
8. Supporters; partners
10. Small amount of color
12. Hit with a sharp blow
13. Careful
16. Madman; lunatic
17. Bothered; annoyed
19. Harsh, grating sound
20. A period of time

Rumble Fish Vocabulary Crossword 3

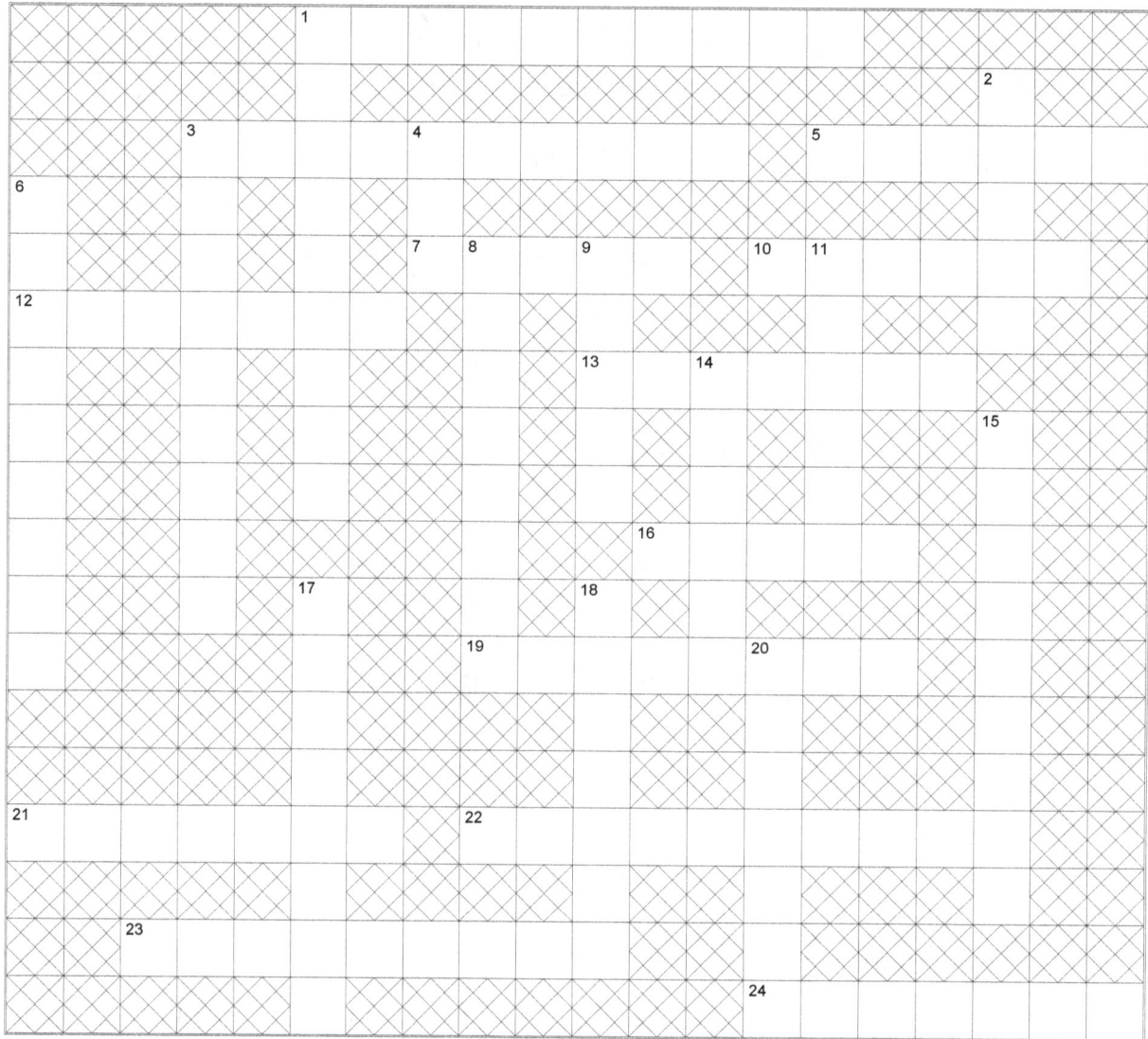

Across
1. Searching
3. Insight
5. Inherited; inborn
7. Intense
10. Madman; lunatic
12. Put in an unsuitable role
13. New and unusual thing
16. Lively
19. Alone; single
21. In a confused manner
22. High-fashion
23. Deserted; left
24. Anxiety; unease

Down
1. Mocking
2. Person who worships many gods
3. Example for future actions
4. A period of time
6. Imitation
8. Careful
9. Small amount of color
11. Supporters; partners
14. Empty
15. Deformed; twisted out of shape
17. Looking angry by lowering the eyebrows
18. Hit with a sharp blow
20. One who does not believe in God

Rumble Fish Vocabulary Crossword 3 Answer Key

Across
1. Searching
3. Insight
5. Inherited; inborn
7. Intense
10. Madman; lunatic
12. Put in an unsuitable role
13. New and unusual thing
16. Lively
19. Alone; single
21. In a confused manner
22. High-fashion
23. Deserted; left
24. Anxiety; unease

Down
1. Mocking
2. Person who worships many gods
3. Example for future actions
4. A period of time
6. Imitation
8. Careful
9. Small amount of color
11. Supporters; partners
14. Empty
15. Deformed; twisted out of shape
17. Looking angry by lowering the eyebrows
18. Hit with a sharp blow
20. One who does not believe in God

Answers

Across: 1. SCROUNGING, 3. PERCEPTION, 5. INNATE, 7. ACUTE, 10. MANIAC, 12. MISCAST, 13. NOVELTY, 16. SASSY, 19. SOLITARY, 21. DAZEDLY, 22. SUPERELITE, 23. ABANDONED, 24. TENSION

Down: 1. SIMULATED, 2. POLYGAMIST (PAGAN?), 3. PRECEDENT, 4. ERA, 6. SARCASTIC, 8. CAUTIOUS, 9. TINGE, 11. ALLIES, 14. VACANT, 15. DISTORTED, 17. SCOWLING, 18. CONKED, 20. ATHEIST

Rumble Fish Vocabulary Crossword 4

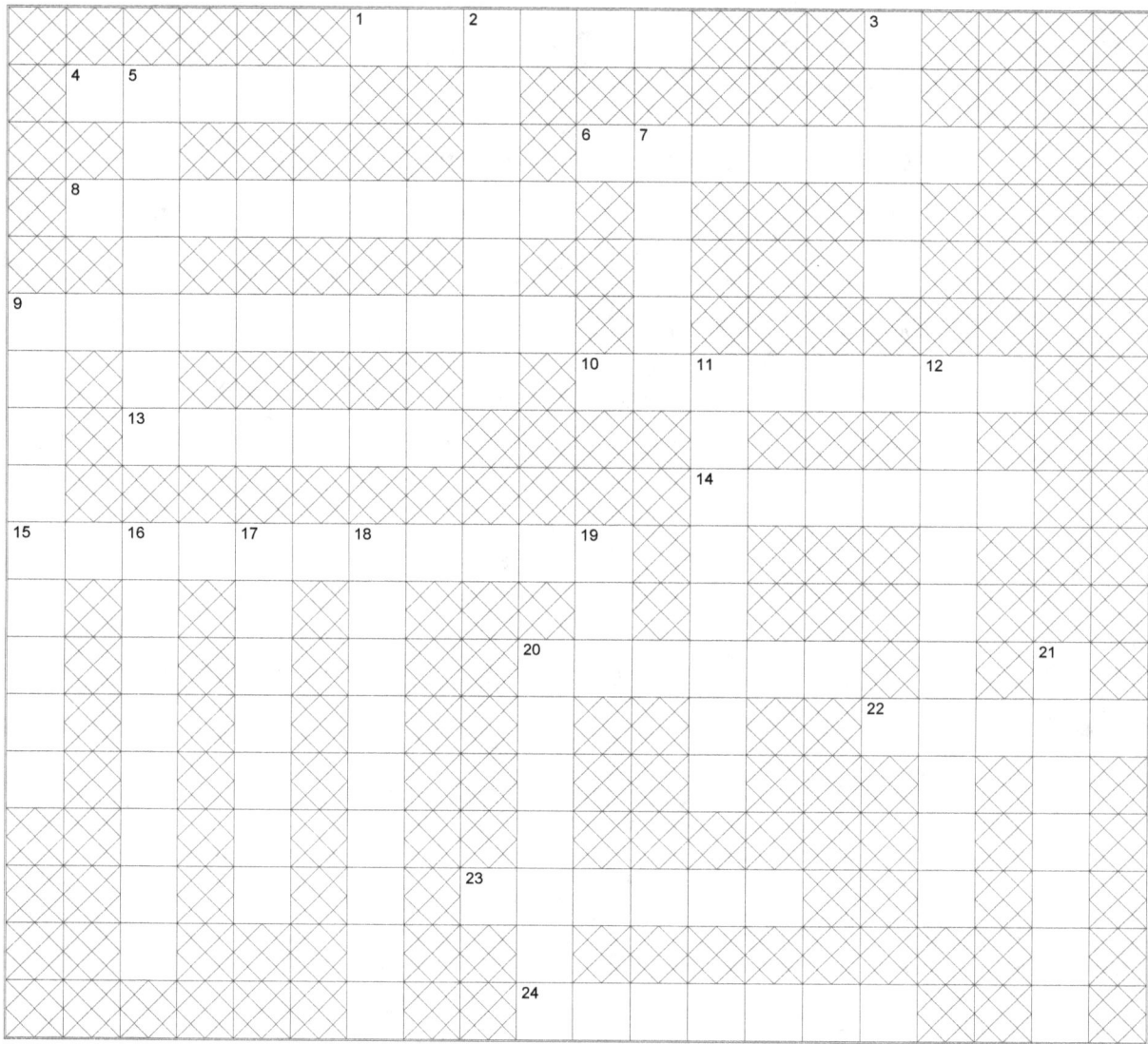

Across
1. Inherited; inborn
4. Intense
6. One who does not believe in God
8. Deformed; twisted out of shape
9. High-fashion
10. Bothered; annoyed
13. Napping
14. Supporters; partners
15. Choice
20. Madman; lunatic
22. Person who worships many gods
23. Empty
24. Anxiety; unease

Down
2. New and unusual thing
3. Lively
5. Hit with a sharp blow
7. Small amount of color
9. Mocking
11. Walking in an angry manner
12. Finally
16. Permit; endure
17. Harsh, grating sound
18. Deserted; left
19. A period of time
20. Put in an unsuitable role
21. In a confused manner

Rumble Fish Vocabulary Crossword 4 Answer Key

Across
1. Inherited; inborn
4. Intense
6. One who does not believe in God
8. Deformed; twisted out of shape
9. High-fashion
10. Bothered; annoyed
13. Napping
14. Supporters; partners
15. Choice
20. Madman; lunatic
22. Person who worships many gods
23. Empty
24. Anxiety; unease

Down
2. New and unusual thing
3. Lively
5. Hit with a sharp blow
7. Small amount of color
9. Mocking
11. Walking in an angry manner
12. Finally
16. Permit; endure
17. Harsh, grating sound
18. Deserted; left
19. A period of time
20. Put in an unsuitable role
21. In a confused manner

Rumble Fish Vocabulary Juggle Letters 1

1. STNEONI = 1. _____
   Anxiety; unease

2. LZDAEDY = 2. _____
   In a confused manner

3. NBBROIHGT = 3. _____
   Aching

4. RAE = 4. _____
   A period of time

5. ERAOLETT = 5. _____
   Permit; endure

6. TOSTDIRED = 6. _____
   Deformed; twisted out of shape

7. SSAYS = 7. _____
   Lively

8. NIDOZG = 8. _____
   Napping

9. CASISMT = 9. _____
   Put in an unsuitable role

10. LIUSDMTAE =10. _____
    Imitation

11. AAPGN =11. _____
    Person who worships many gods

12. IRUEEETLSP =12. _____
    High-fashion

13. THTEIAS =13. _____
    One who does not believe in God

14. WOCSLGIN =14. _____
    Looking angry by lowering the eyebrows

15. RMPVIEIIT =15. _____
    Uncivilized; simple

Rumble Fish Vocabulary Juggle Letters 1 Answer Key

1. STNEONI = 1. TENSION
   Anxiety; unease

2. LZDAEDY = 2. DAZEDLY
   In a confused manner

3. NBBROIHGT = 3. THROBBING
   Aching

4. RAE = 4. ERA
   A period of time

5. ERAOLETT = 5. TOLERATE
   Permit; endure

6. TOSTDIRED = 6. DISTORTED
   Deformed; twisted out of shape

7. SSAYS = 7. SASSY
   Lively

8. NIDOZG = 8. DOZING
   Napping

9. CASISMT = 9. MISCAST
   Put in an unsuitable role

10. LIUSDMTAE = 10. SIMULATED
    Imitation

11. AAPGN = 11. PAGAN
    Person who worships many gods

12. IRUEEETLSP = 12. SUPERELITE
    High-fashion

13. THTEIAS = 13. ATHEIST
    One who does not believe in God

14. WOCSLGIN = 14. SCOWLING
    Looking angry by lowering the eyebrows

15. RMPVIEIIT = 15. PRIMITIVE
    Uncivilized; simple

Rumble Fish Vocabulary Juggle Letters 2

1. NTAINE = 1. _____
   Inherited; inborn

2. ATEOTLER = 2. _____
   Permit; endure

3. RITSCSCAA = 3. _____
   Mocking

4. EDABNNDAO = 4. _____
   Deserted; left

5. ITEGN = 5. _____
   Small amount of color

6. ILAKSGTN = 6. _____
   Walking in an angry manner

7. NIAMCA = 7. _____
   Madman; lunatic

8. ITIIERVMP = 8. _____
   Uncivilized; simple

9. ONIESTN = 9. _____
   Anxiety; unease

10. LISDEATUM =10. _____
    Imitation

11. TIOSCUUA =11. _____
    Careful

12. TRAONRCY =12. _____
    Opposite

13. EIALNVTREAT =13. _____
    Choice

14. LNLEUYAVTE =14. _____
    Finally

15. ESRTPDEE =15. _____
    Bothered; annoyed

Rumble Fish Vocabulary Juggle Letters 2 Answer Key

1. NTAINE   = 1. INNATE
                      Inherited; inborn

2. ATEOTLER   = 2. TOLERATE
                      Permit; endure

3. RITSCSCAA   = 3. SARCASTIC
                      Mocking

4. EDABNNDAO   = 4. ABANDONED
                      Deserted; left

5. ITEGN   = 5. TINGE
                      Small amount of color

6. ILAKSGTN   = 6. STALKING
                      Walking in an angry manner

7. NIAMCA   = 7. MANIAC
                      Madman; lunatic

8. ITIIERVMP   = 8. PRIMITIVE
                      Uncivilized; simple

9. ONIESTN   = 9. TENSION
                      Anxiety; unease

10. LISDEATUM   =10. SIMULATED
                      Imitation

11. TIOSCUUA   =11. CAUTIOUS
                      Careful

12. TRAONRCY   =12. CONTRARY
                      Opposite

13. EIALNVTREAT   =13. ALTERNATIVE
                      Choice

14. LNLEUYAVTE   =14. EVENTUALLY
                      Finally

15. ESRTPDEE   =15. PESTERED
                      Bothered; annoyed

Rumble Fish Vocabulary Juggle Letters 3

1. ICGWSLON = 1. _____
   Looking angry by lowering the eyebrows

2. UAILDTSEM = 2. _____
   Imitation

3. DZEDALY = 3. _____
   In a confused manner

4. SASYS = 4. _____
   Lively

5. GRNGOSNUCI = 5. _____
   Searching

6. NOIOOSBUX = 6. _____
   Offensive; annoying

7. PTOPREENCI = 7. _____
   Insight

8. EYANTLEVUL = 8. _____
   Finally

9. AKTGNISL = 9. _____
   Walking in an angry manner

10. AITENN = 10. _____
    Inherited; inborn

11. ORNGHTBBI = 11. _____
    Aching

12. ACLDMCETIOP = 12. _____
    Difficult; involved

13. IETNG = 13. _____
    Small amount of color

14. RTPSEEED = 14. _____
    Bothered; annoyed

15. ANGPA = 15. _____
    Person who worships many gods

Rumble Fish Vocabulary Juggle Letters 3 Answer Key

1. ICGWSLON = 1. SCOWLING
Looking angry by lowering the eyebrows

2. UAILDTSEM = 2. SIMULATED
Imitation

3. DZEDALY = 3. DAZEDLY
In a confused manner

4. SASYS = 4. SASSY
Lively

5. GRNGOSNUCI = 5. SCROUNGING
Searching

6. NOIOOSBUX = 6. OBNOXIOUS
Offensive; annoying

7. PTOPREENCI = 7. PERCEPTION
Insight

8. EYANTLEVUL = 8. EVENTUALLY
Finally

9. AKTGNISL = 9. STALKING
Walking in an angry manner

10. AITENN = 10. INNATE
Inherited; inborn

11. ORNGHTBBI = 11. THROBBING
Aching

12. ACLDMCETIOP = 12. COMPLICATED
Difficult; involved

13. IETNG = 13. TINGE
Small amount of color

14. RTPSEEED = 14. PESTERED
Bothered; annoyed

15. ANGPA = 15. PAGAN
Person who worships many gods

Rumble Fish Vocabulary Juggle Letters 4

1. TDEODTRIS = 1. _____
   Deformed; twisted out of shape

2. TMAICSS = 2. _____
   Put in an unsuitable role

3. ELEUTIRPSE = 3. _____
   High-fashion

4. CATANV = 4. _____
   Empty

5. IRGASNP = 5. _____
   Harsh, grating sound

6. LZAEYDD = 6. _____
   In a confused manner

7. ENEDCTRPE = 7. _____
   Example for future actions

8. ILLEAS = 8. _____
   Supporters; partners

9. ICRSTAACS = 9. _____
   Mocking

10. NRIVTLTAAEE =10. _____
    Choice

11. TSIORLYA =11. _____
    Alone; single

12. PLIDCEP =12. _____
    Hit with a sharp blow

13. PNAGA =13. _____
    Person who worships many gods

14. VRPIEIITM =14. _____
    Uncivilized; simple

15. TERIPPNCEO =15. _____
    Insight

Rumble Fish Vocabulary Juggle Letters 4 Answer Key

1. TDEODTRIS = 1. DISTORTED
Deformed; twisted out of shape

2. TMAICSS = 2. MISCAST
Put in an unsuitable role

3. ELEUTIRPSE = 3. SUPERELITE
High-fashion

4. CATANV = 4. VACANT
Empty

5. IRGASNP = 5. RASPING
Harsh, grating sound

6. LZAEYDD = 6. DAZEDLY
In a confused manner

7. ENEDCTRPE = 7. PRECEDENT
Example for future actions

8. ILLEAS = 8. ALLIES
Supporters; partners

9. ICRSTAACS = 9. SARCASTIC
Mocking

10. NRIVTLTAAEE = 10. ALTERNATIVE
Choice

11. TSIORLYA = 11. SOLITARY
Alone; single

12. PLIDCEP = 12. CLIPPED
Hit with a sharp blow

13. PNAGA = 13. PAGAN
Person who worships many gods

14. VRPIEIITM = 14. PRIMITIVE
Uncivilized; simple

15. TERIPPNCEO = 15. PERCEPTION
Insight

ABANDONED	Deserted; left
ACUTE	Intense
ALLIES	Supporters; partners
ALTERNATIVE	Choice
ATHEIST	One who does not believe in God
CAUTIOUS	Careful

CLIPPED	Hit with a sharp blow
COMPLICATED	Difficult; involved
CONTRARY	Opposite
DAZEDLY	In a confused manner
DISTORTED	Deformed; twisted out of shape
DOZING	Napping

ERA	A period of time
EVENTUALLY	Finally
INNATE	Inherited; inborn
MANIAC	Madman; lunatic
MISCAST	Put in an unsuitable role
NOVELTY	New and unusual thing

OBNOXIOUS	Offensive; annoying
PAGAN	Person who worships many gods
PERCEPTION	Insight
PESTERED	Bothered; annoyed
PRECEDENT	Example for future actions
PRIMITIVE	Uncivilized; simple

RASPING	Harsh, grating sound
SARCASTIC	Mocking
SASSY	Lively
SCOWLING	Looking angry by lowering the eyebrows
SCROUNGING	Searching
SIMULATED	Imitation

SOLITARY	Alone; single
STALKING	Walking in an angry manner
SUPERELITE	High-fashion
TENSION	Anxiety; unease
THROBBING	Aching
TINGE	Small amount of color

TOLERATE	Permit; endure
VACANT	Empty

Rumble Fish Vocabulary

VACANT	PERCEPTION	SIMULATED	CLIPPED	ERA
NOVELTY	SASSY	STALKING	DOZING	SARCASTIC
ALTERNATIVE	CONTRARY	FREE SPACE	TOLERATE	THROBBING
OBNOXIOUS	SUPERELITE	TENSION	PRECEDENT	ACUTE
TINGE	SCROUNGING	PESTERED	SOLITARY	ATHEIST

Rumble Fish Vocabulary

RASPING	DAZEDLY	COMPLICATED	EVENTUALLY	CAUTIOUS
ALLIES	PAGAN	SCOWLING	MANIAC	INNATE
MISCAST	ABANDONED	FREE SPACE	ATHEIST	SOLITARY
PESTERED	SCROUNGING	TINGE	ACUTE	PRECEDENT
TENSION	SUPERELITE	OBNOXIOUS	THROBBING	TOLERATE

Rumble Fish Vocabulary

MISCAST	PERCEPTION	ATHEIST	DOZING	ALTERNATIVE
PRECEDENT	SUPERELITE	PRIMITIVE	COMPLICATED	OBNOXIOUS
CONTRARY	SARCASTIC	FREE SPACE	NOVELTY	THROBBING
EVENTUALLY	SIMULATED	DISTORTED	ABANDONED	ALLIES
ERA	SOLITARY	SCOWLING	TINGE	CLIPPED

Rumble Fish Vocabulary

RASPING	INNATE	VACANT	STALKING	DAZEDLY
TENSION	SASSY	PAGAN	SCROUNGING	TOLERATE
CAUTIOUS	MANIAC	FREE SPACE	CLIPPED	TINGE
SCOWLING	SOLITARY	ERA	ALLIES	ABANDONED
DISTORTED	SIMULATED	EVENTUALLY	THROBBING	NOVELTY

Rumble Fish Vocabulary

TOLERATE	ABANDONED	ERA	SARCASTIC	ALTERNATIVE
SOLITARY	VACANT	CAUTIOUS	STALKING	ALLIES
SIMULATED	PERCEPTION	FREE SPACE	ATHEIST	OBNOXIOUS
PRIMITIVE	SCROUNGING	RASPING	SASSY	SCOWLING
PAGAN	DOZING	CLIPPED	DISTORTED	ACUTE

Rumble Fish Vocabulary

DAZEDLY	INNATE	THROBBING	MISCAST	SUPERELITE
TINGE	MANIAC	NOVELTY	PESTERED	COMPLICATED
EVENTUALLY	PRECEDENT	FREE SPACE	ACUTE	DISTORTED
CLIPPED	DOZING	PAGAN	SCOWLING	SASSY
RASPING	SCROUNGING	PRIMITIVE	OBNOXIOUS	ATHEIST

Rumble Fish Vocabulary

ERA	SCROUNGING	NOVELTY	DAZEDLY	STALKING
VACANT	SUPERELITE	TINGE	TOLERATE	PERCEPTION
ACUTE	DOZING	FREE SPACE	SIMULATED	THROBBING
CLIPPED	MISCAST	COMPLICATED	MANIAC	PRIMITIVE
PRECEDENT	ATHEIST	EVENTUALLY	INNATE	SCOWLING

Rumble Fish Vocabulary

PESTERED	DISTORTED	PAGAN	CAUTIOUS	ALLIES
SOLITARY	ABANDONED	OBNOXIOUS	CONTRARY	TENSION
ALTERNATIVE	SASSY	FREE SPACE	SCOWLING	INNATE
EVENTUALLY	ATHEIST	PRECEDENT	PRIMITIVE	MANIAC
COMPLICATED	MISCAST	CLIPPED	THROBBING	SIMULATED

Rumble Fish Vocabulary

INNATE	ABANDONED	SASSY	PAGAN	ALLIES
CAUTIOUS	RASPING	ACUTE	PRIMITIVE	PERCEPTION
SIMULATED	SCOWLING	FREE SPACE	ALTERNATIVE	COMPLICATED
CONTRARY	SUPERELITE	PESTERED	DISTORTED	ATHEIST
MANIAC	DAZEDLY	ERA	TINGE	DOZING

Rumble Fish Vocabulary

OBNOXIOUS	EVENTUALLY	SCROUNGING	SARCASTIC	THROBBING
STALKING	TENSION	VACANT	SOLITARY	MISCAST
NOVELTY	PRECEDENT	FREE SPACE	DOZING	TINGE
ERA	DAZEDLY	MANIAC	ATHEIST	DISTORTED
PESTERED	SUPERELITE	CONTRARY	COMPLICATED	ALTERNATIVE

Rumble Fish Vocabulary

ALLIES	SCROUNGING	SCOWLING	ATHEIST	ALTERNATIVE
DOZING	EVENTUALLY	VACANT	MISCAST	SARCASTIC
INNATE	COMPLICATED	FREE SPACE	SASSY	NOVELTY
PESTERED	PERCEPTION	TOLERATE	TENSION	CAUTIOUS
THROBBING	TINGE	PAGAN	CLIPPED	ABANDONED

Rumble Fish Vocabulary

ERA	RASPING	DAZEDLY	SIMULATED	ACUTE
PRECEDENT	MANIAC	CONTRARY	SUPERELITE	OBNOXIOUS
PRIMITIVE	SOLITARY	FREE SPACE	ABANDONED	CLIPPED
PAGAN	TINGE	THROBBING	CAUTIOUS	TENSION
TOLERATE	PERCEPTION	PESTERED	NOVELTY	SASSY

Rumble Fish Vocabulary

EVENTUALLY	ALLIES	STALKING	CAUTIOUS	TINGE
SIMULATED	DISTORTED	INNATE	PRECEDENT	TENSION
SOLITARY	SUPERELITE	FREE SPACE	PAGAN	PESTERED
MANIAC	NOVELTY	THROBBING	PERCEPTION	ERA
COMPLICATED	SASSY	CONTRARY	SCROUNGING	MISCAST

Rumble Fish Vocabulary

DOZING	TOLERATE	ABANDONED	DAZEDLY	VACANT
SCOWLING	SARCASTIC	PRIMITIVE	OBNOXIOUS	ACUTE
ALTERNATIVE	RASPING	FREE SPACE	MISCAST	SCROUNGING
CONTRARY	SASSY	COMPLICATED	ERA	PERCEPTION
THROBBING	NOVELTY	MANIAC	PESTERED	PAGAN

Rumble Fish Vocabulary

VACANT	MANIAC	DAZEDLY	ACUTE	SASSY
INNATE	PESTERED	SUPERELITE	PAGAN	PRECEDENT
ATHEIST	THROBBING	FREE SPACE	SCROUNGING	SCOWLING
CAUTIOUS	PERCEPTION	PRIMITIVE	COMPLICATED	SARCASTIC
CONTRARY	NOVELTY	TINGE	RASPING	DOZING

Rumble Fish Vocabulary

ALTERNATIVE	ALLIES	DISTORTED	EVENTUALLY	TENSION
SOLITARY	SIMULATED	OBNOXIOUS	STALKING	ERA
CLIPPED	ABANDONED	FREE SPACE	DOZING	RASPING
TINGE	NOVELTY	CONTRARY	SARCASTIC	COMPLICATED
PRIMITIVE	PERCEPTION	CAUTIOUS	SCOWLING	SCROUNGING

Rumble Fish Vocabulary

ABANDONED	ERA	TINGE	TENSION	SUPERELITE
DAZEDLY	SIMULATED	CAUTIOUS	RASPING	ALLIES
THROBBING	CLIPPED	FREE SPACE	SCOWLING	NOVELTY
ALTERNATIVE	EVENTUALLY	PESTERED	TOLERATE	MANIAC
PRIMITIVE	SCROUNGING	PRECEDENT	CONTRARY	ATHEIST

Rumble Fish Vocabulary

OBNOXIOUS	DISTORTED	PAGAN	SARCASTIC	SASSY
INNATE	MISCAST	SOLITARY	STALKING	ACUTE
PERCEPTION	DOZING	FREE SPACE	ATHEIST	CONTRARY
PRECEDENT	SCROUNGING	PRIMITIVE	MANIAC	TOLERATE
PESTERED	EVENTUALLY	ALTERNATIVE	NOVELTY	SCOWLING

Rumble Fish Vocabulary

VACANT	SUPERELITE	EVENTUALLY	OBNOXIOUS	DISTORTED
ALTERNATIVE	COMPLICATED	ERA	SCOWLING	CLIPPED
MISCAST	MANIAC	FREE SPACE	NOVELTY	SASSY
ATHEIST	CONTRARY	ABANDONED	STALKING	RASPING
TENSION	DAZEDLY	PRIMITIVE	TINGE	SOLITARY

Rumble Fish Vocabulary

PERCEPTION	PESTERED	SIMULATED	ALLIES	PRECEDENT
DOZING	THROBBING	SARCASTIC	INNATE	SCROUNGING
CAUTIOUS	PAGAN	FREE SPACE	SOLITARY	TINGE
PRIMITIVE	DAZEDLY	TENSION	RASPING	STALKING
ABANDONED	CONTRARY	ATHEIST	SASSY	NOVELTY

Rumble Fish Vocabulary

STALKING	TENSION	SCROUNGING	PRECEDENT	DOZING
PERCEPTION	ATHEIST	PESTERED	ERA	COMPLICATED
INNATE	ABANDONED	FREE SPACE	OBNOXIOUS	CONTRARY
SIMULATED	ACUTE	PAGAN	SUPERELITE	NOVELTY
ALLIES	RASPING	SASSY	ALTERNATIVE	SCOWLING

Rumble Fish Vocabulary

TOLERATE	CLIPPED	PRIMITIVE	EVENTUALLY	SARCASTIC
VACANT	MANIAC	SOLITARY	TINGE	DAZEDLY
MISCAST	THROBBING	FREE SPACE	SCOWLING	ALTERNATIVE
SASSY	RASPING	ALLIES	NOVELTY	SUPERELITE
PAGAN	ACUTE	SIMULATED	CONTRARY	OBNOXIOUS

Rumble Fish Vocabulary

VACANT	PESTERED	CAUTIOUS	THROBBING	OBNOXIOUS
TENSION	CONTRARY	ATHEIST	DAZEDLY	SASSY
DISTORTED	RASPING	FREE SPACE	EVENTUALLY	DOZING
MANIAC	PERCEPTION	ALTERNATIVE	ALLIES	SCROUNGING
CLIPPED	PRIMITIVE	SCOWLING	STALKING	SOLITARY

Rumble Fish Vocabulary

ABANDONED	TOLERATE	ERA	COMPLICATED	SUPERELITE
MISCAST	NOVELTY	SIMULATED	INNATE	PAGAN
PRECEDENT	ACUTE	FREE SPACE	SOLITARY	STALKING
SCOWLING	PRIMITIVE	CLIPPED	SCROUNGING	ALLIES
ALTERNATIVE	PERCEPTION	MANIAC	DOZING	EVENTUALLY

Rumble Fish Vocabulary

SUPERELITE	SASSY	ATHEIST	MISCAST	PAGAN
COMPLICATED	ALLIES	SOLITARY	PESTERED	CONTRARY
SIMULATED	PRIMITIVE	FREE SPACE	MANIAC	TENSION
OBNOXIOUS	CAUTIOUS	INNATE	SCROUNGING	ALTERNATIVE
STALKING	PERCEPTION	EVENTUALLY	DISTORTED	DOZING

Rumble Fish Vocabulary

TOLERATE	SARCASTIC	THROBBING	ACUTE	TINGE
NOVELTY	PRECEDENT	CLIPPED	SCOWLING	ERA
DAZEDLY	VACANT	FREE SPACE	DOZING	DISTORTED
EVENTUALLY	PERCEPTION	STALKING	ALTERNATIVE	SCROUNGING
INNATE	CAUTIOUS	OBNOXIOUS	TENSION	MANIAC

Rumble Fish Vocabulary

ALTERNATIVE	ATHEIST	SCOWLING	CAUTIOUS	STALKING
MISCAST	DAZEDLY	TINGE	PRECEDENT	ALLIES
COMPLICATED	ERA	FREE SPACE	NOVELTY	CONTRARY
EVENTUALLY	SIMULATED	PRIMITIVE	PAGAN	THROBBING
TOLERATE	ABANDONED	PERCEPTION	SARCASTIC	DISTORTED

Rumble Fish Vocabulary

SUPERELITE	MANIAC	SOLITARY	CLIPPED	RASPING
PESTERED	SASSY	TENSION	ACUTE	SCROUNGING
OBNOXIOUS	VACANT	FREE SPACE	DISTORTED	SARCASTIC
PERCEPTION	ABANDONED	TOLERATE	THROBBING	PAGAN
PRIMITIVE	SIMULATED	EVENTUALLY	CONTRARY	NOVELTY

Rumble Fish Vocabulary

THROBBING	SUPERELITE	SCOWLING	ATHEIST	NOVELTY
PERCEPTION	VACANT	INNATE	DISTORTED	OBNOXIOUS
SARCASTIC	PAGAN	FREE SPACE	ERA	TOLERATE
SCROUNGING	PRIMITIVE	TENSION	DOZING	CAUTIOUS
SASSY	CONTRARY	SIMULATED	RASPING	PRECEDENT

Rumble Fish Vocabulary

COMPLICATED	MANIAC	ALLIES	TINGE	PESTERED
MISCAST	ACUTE	DAZEDLY	CLIPPED	ABANDONED
STALKING	EVENTUALLY	FREE SPACE	PRECEDENT	RASPING
SIMULATED	CONTRARY	SASSY	CAUTIOUS	DOZING
TENSION	PRIMITIVE	SCROUNGING	TOLERATE	ERA

Rumble Fish Vocabulary

MISCAST	CAUTIOUS	NOVELTY	COMPLICATED	CONTRARY
THROBBING	PRECEDENT	SIMULATED	DAZEDLY	ALTERNATIVE
PAGAN	TOLERATE	FREE SPACE	RASPING	INNATE
SUPERELITE	DOZING	SASSY	PESTERED	SCROUNGING
SCOWLING	SOLITARY	EVENTUALLY	ERA	ABANDONED

Rumble Fish Vocabulary

STALKING	VACANT	PERCEPTION	MANIAC	ACUTE
SARCASTIC	TINGE	ATHEIST	OBNOXIOUS	DISTORTED
PRIMITIVE	TENSION	FREE SPACE	ABANDONED	ERA
EVENTUALLY	SOLITARY	SCOWLING	SCROUNGING	PESTERED
SASSY	DOZING	SUPERELITE	INNATE	RASPING

www.ingramcontent.com/pod-product-compliance
Lightning Source LLC
Chambersburg PA
CBHW081457070526
44586CB00019B/2395